the sixteenth year

AN OPEN ADOPTION MEMOIR

LEAH OUTTEN

KW
KingdomWinds
PUBLISHING

Unless otherwise indicated, all Scripture references are taken from the Holy Bible, New International Version®, NIV® Copyright © 1973, 1978, 1984, 2011 by Biblica, Inc.® Used by permission. All rights reserved worldwide.

First Edition, 2023
ISBN: 978-1-64590-050-4
Published by Kingdom Winds Publishing.
www.kingdomwinds.com
publishing@kingdomwinds.com
Printed in the United States of America.

Table of Contents

To my birth daughter, whose existence changed my path and world for the better. May you know that you are always wanted and loved.

Endorsements

"*The Sixteenth Year* is a powerful book of a birth mom's brave journey to make the choice to place her baby for adoption. Not only will you be inspired by Leah's personal story, you will hear a refreshingly honest perspective of her adoption process beginning from pregnancy, through birth and leading to her bond with her teenage daughter today. Leah's courage is contagious!!"

— Amy Ford, President of Embrace Grace, author of *Help Her Be Brave*

"Her experiences will both inform you and inspire you."

— Melissa Ohden, President of Abortion Survivors Network, author of *You Carried Me*

"Leah is an inspiration to everyone she encounters. She is talented, authentic, and passionate."

— Tori Shaw, President of They Are Not Forgotten, author of *I Had A Secret For Seventeen Years* and *Free Indeed*

Note

The situations and conversations in this book are written as factually as possible based on my memory and according to others who were also present. Some names or places have been changed to protect privacy.

I also realize that this level of open adoption isn't possible for everyone, nor is it best for every circumstance. Open adoption can look different, just as every birth mother's experience varies. This is our story and what worked well for us, but I hope it shows what can be possible.

I do believe in family preservation first and foremost, but when adoption is chosen, I advocate for it to be done well. Unfortunately, the unbiased support you'll read about that I experienced from my family, social worker, community, and even my daughter's adoptive parents is rare. The system is flawed, and somehow I got lucky within it. I share my story to help advocate for better care for expectant moms and birth moms— because our healing matters. When birth parents are loved and supported well, they often are emotionally healthier so that they can have healthy relationships. That benefits adoptees, too. It benefits everyone in the adoption constellation. As more adoptee and birth mom voices are rising to share their experiences, I urge you to listen to them. We can all learn from each other's stories of what to do or what not to do. My story is just one.

Introduction

No one dreams of one day becoming a birth mother. After all, in this American culture, we are not generally looked upon in a positive light. We can be seen as taking the easy way out. Selfish. Greedy. No one wakes up and says, "I'm going to become a birth mother!" with excitement.

In reality, becoming a birth mother is a slow progression and a devastating choice, a domino effect of one thing leading to another caused by choices of our own making, actions done to us, or a complex combination crashing into one after another after another. Then there is no other choice but to fall.

Yet, it was falling, toppling under the weight of my sin, that helped me to finally look up for help and see Jesus' kind eyes waiting for me. That was the real domino effect: the process of falling so far that all I could do was look up. When I did, I found a God who loves me deeply, even when I felt so undeserving, and who sought to stand me upright again. This time, doing things His way.

For redemption to take place, there has to be a fall. There has to be an end of ourselves and of our own efforts before He can make something new in His way. For me, that was my sixteenth year.

HOW DID I GET HERE?

"When we chase happiness externally, we're simply looking for God in all the wrong places."
— **Gabrielle Bernstein**[1]

---

1 Bernstein, Gabrielle. Miracles Now: 108 Life-Changing Tools for Less Stress, More Flow, and Finding Your True Purpose. Hay House, Inc. 2014. p. 7.

CHAPTER 1

Looking for Love

In a teeny college town in the mountains of North Carolina, I was born to two parents who barely knew each other. I was an unplanned pregnancy myself. Adoption was even considered for me at one point, but my mother, Evelyn, chose to parent me as a single mother. When I was pulled into the world, she figured I was her one chance at being a mom. Forceps left a scar on my cheek as a reminder of her hard labor that September 11th, 1987, day. My newborn pictures have a screaming crimson gash next to my yellow pacifier to mark my stubbornly late arrival. My father, Vic, was a senior in college when I was born. I arrived into this world while he was taking his Spanish exam, and he rushed to see me at the hospital nearby as soon as he could.

Though my parents were not together for long, I am grateful I still had them both in my life in their own ways. My mom was my primary parent for most of my childhood. She worked hard to finish her degree and state license to provide for us. She aimed to provide me with opportunities that she didn't have growing up. She has always been my biggest fan and encouraged me to chase my dreams, whatever that was at the moment. My dad made efforts to see me whenever he could, even after graduating college

13

and moving a few hours away to build stability in his hometown. Eventually, our time turned into scheduled shared holidays, weeks spent together in the summer, and every other weekend during the school year. Overall, though, it wasn't an easy or joyful childhood, to be quite honest. There were certainly good memories and giggles, fun trips, and making the best of things, but I held a deep sadness at my core.

My mom taught me a love for hiking adventures even as a tiny three-year-old, a love for concerts, an appreciation for journaling feelings, and creating art. I know she did the best she could, given her own deficits in her family growing up. She could not give me what she had not received herself.

We bounced from house to house, moving often as she found new opportunities to provide for us or for me to be closer to my dad. My family all described me as quiet until I got out of my shell, and I still can be like that. I did well in school, often making the honor roll and earning "Terrific Kid" awards. I aimed to make people smile; I wanted to be liked. Despite moving often, I easily made good friends no matter where we lived. They were rays of sunshine peeking out of the gloomy clouded sky of my childhood.

One day in elementary school, it occurred to me that I was different from my friends. In the 1990's, divorce wasn't as common as it is now; I didn't know *anyone* with separate households at that time. Just me. Worst of all, my mom and dad weren't even divorced; they'd never truly been together. Did that make me a burden? An outsider? Did it make me unloved and unwanted? Did this make *me* shameful? These are questions I wrestled with internally, and I desperately sought love and approval to prove otherwise.

My dad married my stepmom, Cyndi, when I was five years old, but her warm hugs and adoration have been around for as long as I can remember. Her family embraced me as their own too, providing me with an atmosphere of cozy acceptance when I was visiting. A family that is not biologically mine became a close emotional connection, which made me feel loved and cherished in their presence.

I treasured those visits. It was an escape, a glimpse at what a happy family could look like with a solid, secure attachment. My dad would snuggle me as we read books before bedtime. Cyndi would sing me "The Rainbow Connection" and rub my forehead as I drifted off to sleep. They would take me shopping for new clothes and toys. My cousin and I would have matching Christmas plaid pajamas and slippers with Santa's head on them. My Pawpaw, Cyndi's dad, would buy my favorite Peach Buds candy to let me know that he was thinking of me while I was away. My Nanny, Cyndi's mom, would sew me outfits by hand. One of them was a blue and white striped dress with red gummy bears as the buttons that my youngest daughter now wears. The environment was always so thoughtful and welcoming. I felt wanted and safe in their arms. I felt like they took authentic delight in who I was.

In contrast, when living with my mom, it was often just the two of us. She was exhausted from working a full-time job while also in school. And while I understand that now, I often felt lonely. I remember playing board games being both myself and an imaginary player when my mom couldn't play and watching *a lot* of television. I struggled to understand why I felt such anger boiling within me. Now I know that the anger bursting from my tantrums towards my mom was sadness. I wanted what I perceived to be a normal family, happy and together like my friends had. I wanted to feel seen and loved. At times I wanted to live with my dad, but I never said a word out of fear of hurting my mom, only expressing my feelings through tantrums.

A majority of my memories as a young child living with my mom are in daycares or with babysitters. Did I have fun and make good friends? Of course. But I also missed my mom; I just wanted to be with her. I wanted to have my mom pick me up right after school and not need to ride the bus or attend after-school care. These feelings intensified because it was in the care of others that my life took a twisted turn.

The memories still engulf and impact me today when they resurface, though therapy has been helpful. I was sexually molested by two men at separate times, that I can remember, between the ages of three and five. The perverted choices of others stole my innocence and awakened curiosities that shouldn't have been awake yet. In a time of vulnerability and needing protection, I was easily trusting, seeking the love and security I desired, yet I was robbed. Of course, as a petite, blonde-haired olive-skinned girl, I didn't know it was wrong. I thought I was loved and special in this perverse narrative. This secret burrowed deeper into the soil of my heart, threatening to grow its prickly thorns as the years passed—and it did. It would be many years before I realized the truth and began to rip out the weed someone else planted to begin healing.

This abuse coupled with my early years also may have been why I was boy crazy. Even in kindergarten, I chased boys around the playground hoping to capture attention. However, in eighth grade when my mom met and quickly married my stepdad, I spiraled deeper into seeking attention from boys. Falling into depression as my home life shifted, I sought approval and control in the outside world.

Maybe it was a rebellion to express my disapproval. Maybe it was coping or survival. As I went into high school, seeking value and what I thought was love from others became an obsession. I always had crushes and often had boyfriends. I would say "yes" to boys that I didn't even really find cute simply because I liked the idea of being desired. Eventually, that led to boys taking advantage of me, and I let them. I didn't know my own inherent value and worth. I've always wanted to be liked, remember? It wasn't likable to say no. I thought I was going along with things because I wanted to, but looking back, I realize I made the choices I did simply to keep feeling valuable. The shame swallowed me as my worth actually diminished more, yet I kept on.

The void within me I was seeking to satisfy would be filled for a time by one relationship or another in a cruel illusion that I would be happy for a time. Before long, I'd be cast aside and rejected, too clingy for them, or they had moved on to the next girl. Of course, this trampled any worth I thought I had acquired, so I kept looking for the next "fix," so to speak. I used this time in the most unhealthy way to steal back the power taken from me as a little girl. Realizing my looks had power over others to gain attention and connection, even for a brief time, I used it. In doing so, little pieces of my heart chipped off here and there, not even considering how that would affect my future marriage or my self-worth.

The illusion of fulfillment was there, always fooling me for a time; but reality never failed to assert itself with a swish of its hand to sling shame back at me. *What am I doing? What have I done?* I was spiraling internally– torn between the highs and lows of it all. Still, I pressed on.

Trying out different versions of me depending on who I was with at the time was thrilling, and if nothing else, it widened my view of the world. There was too much freedom in those teenage years, too many compromises made or turning a blind eye. Each year, each boy, each internal cry for love and attention was another domino falling.

Samuel sat behind me freshman year in Mr. Gaines's Honors English class. I had known of him since sixth grade as he was my crush's best friend back then, but we had never spoken until that day. Perhaps he saw this as his chance to finally talk to me, as unbeknownst to me at the time, I had been his crush for years.

He wasn't exactly my type, and I had my eye on another person at the time anyway. In middle school, he played in the band and was in the chess club. He was very smart and always in advanced classes. Samuel wore a blonde bowl cut above his crystal blue eyes and was still awkwardly growing, like most of us at fourteen and fifteen years old. With my people-pleasing tendencies and a drive to want to do well plus a love for reading, I listened intently to Mr. Gaines as we discussed classic literature.

Samuel had other plans. He would pass me notes and make me laugh at the worst times. I was not a troublemaker in class, but Samuel caused us to get caught a few times as he kept trying to get my attention. The roles were reversed in the attention-getting, and it felt weird. Eventually, Mr. Gaines separated us, and I was relieved to focus on my work in peace.

Still, he pursued me. It was rather sweet at times, I will say. One day he waited outside my Algebra class with a giant pixie stick he had bought me. Trying his hardest to woo me that semester, I still was not interested. I continued to date other boys, and Samuel remained in the friend zone.

At the end of freshman year, he wrote in my yearbook, "I wish that we could have been closer. Call me sometime this summer, and maybe we can do something. -Samuel" The disappointment was obvious, and I admit even I was confused why I didn't like him back in the way he liked me. He was sweet. He was giving me the perceived value I had always wanted, but it felt too much. It felt relentless, smothering.

Over the summer, we did talk occasionally, and while I was on vacation, he discovered what hotel I was staying in. My uncle handed me the phone. "Hello?" I answered with embarrassment, perhaps expecting my mom to be the voice on the line. It was Samuel. He called every evening that week to talk, racking up a huge phone bill for my aunt and uncle to pay.

As sophomore year began, I kept him at arm's length once more, but my interest was piqued when he showed up with a new haircut and clothes. He had grown over the summer. There were new boyfriends and interests occupying my mind, though. As a competitive dancer, I spent a lot of my time in practices after school, and one of my best friends, Melanie, had invited me to her church and youth group (admittedly, I often went to see a boy there, too). In those months, God was planting seeds of faith to be watered later.

When Greg Laurie's Harvest Crusade came to town, I joined my church friends in attending. I had never seen such passionate excitement over Jesus before as worship music played and Greg spoke Biblical hope over the crowd. At the end of the night, people began filing down the stairs to be saved on the coliseum floor. Feeling the pull within my soul to go down there too, to be a part of this kind of crowd that seemed so full of joy and hope, I wrestled within. My soul wanted to fly to freedom, but my body felt like lead in my seat. Still, it sparked a deeper curiosity about Jesus, and I told Melanie that night, "I want a faith like that."

My experiences with God growing up had been listening to Christian radio, begrudgingly going to church with my dad on my weekend visits, praying only before holiday meals, and a few weeks at a YMCA summer camp where God felt tangibly close. Those seeds were there waiting in the darkness of my soul, waiting for light and water to seep into them to sprout.

I went home after the Harvest Crusade with a desire to change and to know God's love like I saw others experience there. In the computer glow of my room that night, I sent Matt from school an AIM message because I knew he had a deep faith. In the rectangle box of our conversation screen, he walked me through the sinner's prayer. While I may not have been a hundred percent all-in yet, there certainly was a new growing tension between Jesus and the secular world I was drowning in. It would take more heartache for my faith to deeply take root.

Little changes within me did happen as I became more aware of God's Word, and I felt more conviction. The music I blasted from my room more often was now Superchick and Toby Mac rather than the angrier Sum41 and Avril Lavigne. My soul was searching for something else to help me fill my emptiness. I related to songs that spoke to the internal frustrations I felt, like DC Talk's "In The Light." I despised my own behavior. I wanted to do better, to be better, but I felt stuck. I kept attending church with my friends. My aunt gave me a magazine Bible that presented God's word in a youthful and interesting way, along with a golden cross necklace at Christmas time. My dad's side of the family was thrilled for me, but I felt caught between the "good girl" I wanted to be and the life I was actually living.

Boys, appearances, and seeking to fill my void in all the wrong ways still had a hold on me, even with my curiosity about Jesus. So, when the boy from youth group made it obvious he wasn't going to dump his girlfriend for me, I turned to the one who was still there wanting my attention: Samuel.

He came over to hang out with Melanie and me on New Year's Eve as we rang in the year 2003. He brought yet another gift for me and begged for a kiss at midnight. I can't remember if I obliged his request then, if so, it must have been incredibly awkward. Yet from that night, things shifted, and I decided to give him a chance. I allowed myself to finally be wooed by his charm.

He had just turned sixteen, and I was fifteen when we started dating that January. With his birthday came a license and a new-to-him black Jeep with a big red bow on top. For us, it was freedom. We quickly became inseparable, feeling the rush of independence as he drove us around town with the windows down and music blaring. I often would ride home from school with him because being with him was better than my dreary quiet home or fighting with my mom. He came from a split home as well, and we most often hung out at his dad's condo. We would watch television all afternoon (he loved cartoons), and he would cook for us. Chicken Alfredo and frozen pepperoni pizza were common staples for us in those winter and spring afternoons.

Thursday, February 13th, my stepdad answered the door with me following close behind, curious who it was, as we didn't have visitors pop in often. "It's for you," he muttered. Red roses appeared at my door with "I love you" on the card.

"I sent them a day early so you would be surprised," Samuel told me on the phone.

On Friday for the real Valentine's Day, he took me to the mall, and we went to Build-a-Bear for my gift. It was a white bear with red paws and nose, a special holiday bear. In the red heart nose and paws were magnets that would stick together like it was blowing a kiss. Before stuffing the bear, the store attendant directed him to hop around the store floor proclaiming his love for me. Giggling out of embarrassment and endeared that he would make a fool out of himself for me, I fell even harder for him right there.

"He's a keeper, honey!" the attendant told me with a grin.

In February, he also invited me to a dance at his church, a purity ball. Which was ironic as we were pure in God's eyes no longer. He gave me a gold rose ring to fit on my ring finger that evening sitting in the back of his mama's car. He was able to perfectly guess my size. I took it as another sign of his care and love for me. Samuel treated me with adoration in the early days. We passed folded notes back and forth through the school days, each one assuring that he loved me and would always be there for me.

Sharing a kitchen with him, watching him interact with his little cousins, and responsibly doing chores his dad asked of him gave me hope for a future together for a time. He seemed like a solid, good-hearted choice. Though I was young, I knew I wanted to get married and have a family one day. I was already looking for those clues of who would be a good fit for the life I wanted to create. Those months were a glimpse at what could be the happy, love-filled family life I had desired as a little girl.

As the school year ended, however, we were drifting apart into summer. My internal struggles were raging war within me to stop how I was living my life despite the happy moments I felt. I would have panic attacks that caused visual disturbances as guilt gripped my conscience. On the other hand, he was beginning to be caught up with a different crowd and began smoking pot. Partying, smoking, and drinking were never appealing to me, and it caused a large tension between us. He became callused and uncaring when I shared my concerns that he was changing, so we agreed to take a break.

Like magnets drawn together, we couldn't stay apart for long. In between my summer flings and camp weeks, we still found one another. It was hard to think of him with someone else, yet I always had another boy to fill the gaps in my time.

Even my mother sat me down on our cream-swirled couch that summer and said, "Leah, don't you think you're stringing too many boys along?"

In my juvenile mind, I was just having fun; isn't that what being a teenager is about? The weight of guilt was pulling me down, though. I lost my passion for dance and quit the team suddenly. I couldn't fake a smile anymore or leap across the floor with the light-heartedness that I used to have. Darkness, a warning, was creeping in, but I didn't listen. I wanted to keep doing things my way.

September 11th, 2003 was my sixteenth birthday. I had a small family party at my dad's house over the weekend, and they gifted me with real diamond earrings to mark this special milestone. Jessica, another close friend, came for the weekend to celebrate with me. None of us knew how our lives would change in the coming month.

Samuel and I had kept being pulled back together as junior year of high school began, but it was never again what it used to be. He had chosen his path, and I was left clinging to what I wished it could have been and who he used to be. Still, one September day when he decided to flirt with me, I went to lunch and skipped a class, the one and only day I ever did such a thing, to be with him. *Why do I keep going back?* I remember the thrill it felt to be rebellious that day and the hope my heart still hung onto that we could work it out.

That decision would change our life as the dominos kept racing forward.

CHAPTER 2

Two Lines and the Aftermath

This wasn't any trip to Walmart to pick up more notebook paper for class or only to get a snack for our sleepover that night. It was a sneaky endeavor with little white lies told to cover our tracks and convince adults of the help we— I— needed. Samuel wouldn't take me to get a test, and I didn't want to alert my mom if it wasn't needed yet, so Jessica was helping me on this mission. We needed a ride, and we needed money. Thankfully Jessica's grandparents easily agreed to our request for a Saturday night sleepover and to stop for snacks before heading to their house. They handed us some cash to pay and now waited in the car with their windows down feeling the crisp October air while we ran in to acquire our goodies.

Jessica and I wandered up the white glossy linoleum floors divided into aisles. The glare of the tubed lights moved along with us, and I felt watched. Exposed. Vulnerable in my walk of shame. What if someone saw me? My palms were sweaty, and my heartbeat rammed audibly within my chest. We walked briskly as we sought the package we were looking for. My white Adidas with gray stripes squeaked as we turned to find the aisle, the one that held the answer to whether I could allow myself to stop worrying or to worry even more. My period was two weeks late, and I knew something was up. Every internet search and cucumber with ranch craving since then pointed to the idea that I was pregnant.

I was so grateful that Jessica was with me; I couldn't have completed this mission alone. Samuel and I were in an off-again phase; I couldn't depend on him. Jessica was my best friend since the first day of seventh grade. She had become a constant sidekick in my life even though she had moved schools. Sleepovers a few times a month were the norm; her family had become family to me and vice versa. We had bonded over both being extra short in stature (fun size, you might say), having split homes, moving often, and having half-siblings whom we adored. Jessica had a blonde bob while I had chestnut brown hair that was finally growing down my back after a horrible decision to cut it too short in ninth grade. She was louder and feisty, making her opinion well-known. I was quiet and leaned into her courage to boost my own in a lot of ways. She wasn't afraid to tell me hard things I needed to hear or encourage me when I needed it. I knew that night I would need that more than ever.

We slowed the pace as we searched, my eyes darting from different kinds of feminine hygiene products to the area I usually tried to ignore out of sheer awkwardness. Today I could not ignore it. There they were: pregnancy tests. Shelves filled with colorful rectangular boxes with plastic sticks inside all proclaiming to be 99.99% accurate.

"They all do the same thing, right? What do I get?" I asked Jessica as I picked up a box and read the back. Her mom had recently had a baby, and I figured she might have a clue.

"Just go with the cheapest, I guess. We don't have a lot of money and still need to buy snacks like we said we were," she replied.

I picked up the Walmart brand with pink plastered all over it, the cheapest of them all. That $3.88 box would change my life.

After grabbing what typical slumber party snacks we could still afford, we walked to the register. Jessica placed the box on the belt leading to the cashier while I added our other items. She was always the bolder one, never afraid of anything in my eyes. I'm too embarrassed to even take ownership of that box; how immature is that? Here I am possibly pregnant, and I rely on others to pay for what is mine. I felt mortified that I could have a tiny life within me that would depend on me while I was still very dependent on others, even to get a ride to the store and pay. I was too immature to even face a cashier's curious or judgmental gaze, but I didn't know what her eyes held because I never dared to look into them.

When we got back to her grandparents' green sedan, dusk curtained down behind the clouds. I was thankful that in the dim light, they wouldn't easily see what my blue sheer bag contained. As we wound the country road to their house, gravel crunching beneath us and dust flying behind us, I couldn't help but open the package. I flipped on the backseat light, discreetly holding the package within the bag. I've always had a fascination with reading instructions, and the anticipation was killing me. Reading was one small thing I could do to pass the time, and I wanted to absorb all the information I could to make sure I did the test correctly later. I observed the tiny clock graphic saying to wait three minutes to read the results; that seemed fair. Then I saw that it suggested waiting until morning for the best results. I slumped in disappointment; I needed an answer now, not in the morning. Did I really need to wait even longer than I had already?

Later that evening after dinner and watching "Serendipity" for the tenth time together, the anticipation got to me. By then, it was nearing midnight, her grandparents had gone to bed, and the house was filled with quiet darkness aside from the television's glow.

"I can't wait anymore. I need to know! I know I won't be able to sleep unless I take the test," I huffed as I stood up quickly and grabbed the box I had hidden in my sleepover supplies.

We tiptoed to the bathroom as to not disturb the sleeping house. I read the directions yet again, and this time the three-minute wait seemed impossibly unfair, an eternity. I wanted instant results. Two weeks of questioning and researching and worrying had crescendoed to this moment. I was finally going to know.

But then, do I really want to know? Maybe if I don't take a test, it won't be true? I took a deep breath and exhaled anxiety into the small bathroom. Jessica stood with her back to me as I followed the instructions. I didn't have to wait very long: within three seconds the positive line appeared to confirm my suspicions. Two distinct pink lines gave me my answer.

"Oh my gosh," Jessica said with stunned eyes as she bent over to look at the results on the counter. She gave me a hug and whispered, "I'm sorry."

My thoughts swirled around like mist twirling and swaying in all directions, unsure of where to go. Should I be happy? Sad? Upset? I was painfully aware of my shortcomings as a young mother. I didn't even have my driver's license yet. No job. A junior in high school. The more I thought of what I lacked, the more my mind swirled. And what would my parents say? I vaguely heard Jessica comfort me and tell me that I wasn't alone. Babies are happy things, I rationalized. In this moment, the mental mist cleared as I chose to push aside the fears and worries for now. In that instant, love for the tiny baby inside me grew tremendously.

Jessica and I stayed up late by the light of the computer screen, wondering if the little one inside me would be a boy or girl. On Baby Center's website, we entered the information needed to discover my due date: June 11th, 2004. It seemed like an eternity away. I was six weeks along, and the picture showed a baby the size of a tiny lentil. How amazing.

We giggled at the thought of my tiny frame with a round protruding baby belly and discussed what could possibly fit me and still look cute. We looked up baby names and nursery decorations. We dreamed together about the exciting and adorable things we would get to do with this baby. I imagined gently rocking the baby to sleep and feeding him or her as I looked into my baby's eyes with love and care. I imagined a toddler running into my room as I finished up homework. I dared to even imagine us as a family of three. I hadn't yet been able to reach Samuel, though. Where is he?

Jessica and I focused on the good things, the happy things, that night as I processed this shift in life. I guess I needed that for one night. I needed to sit in the nativity of young motherhood and not face yet the hardships surely to come. Finally exhausted in the unseen dark hours of the night, we curled up in a shared twin bed facing opposite directions. I remember rolling to my side and falling asleep with a hand on my still small stomach, hoping my love seeped through. I wanted to give this baby what I always desired—love.

Lying in bed the next morning, I reached down to the floor and took out the test from the box again. Feeling the smooth plastic, I checked for two lines again. Yep, they were still there. Two pink lines. Two parallel lines, like two roads leading to two different worlds. Two choices. Worry crept in along with the morning light through the window. The night before was filled with hopes and dreams, but what would reality bring? What will my parents say? Will they disown me, kick me out? What about college? What will Samuel say? Will he stick around? How was I going to provide for my baby and myself? Will my parents help? My worries morphed into the reality that I was 16 and pregnant. What was I going to do now?

The first step was telling Samuel. Jessica's Pawpaw brought us to her dad's house that Sunday, giving me more time to make a plan with Jessica before seeing my mom. I dialed Samuel's number from memory on their cordless house phone, finally getting a hold of him to tell him our news. He didn't have much to say and had friends over, so we quickly hung up. Hot frustration crept up my neck as I saw yet again how he had changed; I was no longer a priority, and neither would this baby be. Where was the guy who, in all those notes earlier this year, promised to be there for me. Where was he when I really needed him?

"He's a jerk. I never liked him anyway. You'll be fine without him," Jessica comforted me. "So... how are you going to tell your mom?"

We laid on Jessica's bed facing the ceiling, pondering my next move in life like a game of chess.

"I don't know... her birthday is Thursday. I can't ruin her birthday. Maybe I'll wait? But I don't know if I can keep this secret and pretend I'm fine."

No words I considered seemed right. How would I break this earth-shattering news to my family's little world?

When my mom came to pick me up, I did keep my secret a little longer, but by Monday afternoon, the guilt and shame were trickling down my face. I could pretend no more. Hearing her car door slam shut outside, I placed myself where I knew she would see me, right on the couch by the front door. As soon as she saw my teary state, she dropped everything in her hands and rushed to sit with me.

"Leah! What's wrong?"

But no words came, just gut-wrenching sobs. Heaving and gasping for each breath I took, I grasped for the words but found none. She began guessing what was wrong. I shook my head no over and over until she hit the jackpot.

"Are you... pregnant?" I shook my head yes with my eyes sealed shut, afraid to look at the reaction on her face. She hugged me, "Are you sure?" I showed her the test I had taken with Jessica. I was sure. "Well, I thought your period seemed late," she replied with a sigh. She didn't berate me or shame me as I had braced myself for. She only asked questions to clarify my situation and remained calm, gentle with her words, which helped me to calm down as well.

The next day she had me take another test. I knew it would be positive right away, too. Quickly my mom went into action making doctor and counseling appointments and setting up Medicaid. With my secret out with one parent, I breathed a little easier, but I had two more parents and a whole lot of other family to tell.

I didn't though; I kept waiting. It was easier to avoid revealing the truth of my actions when I didn't see the rest of my family every day like I did my mom. Disappointing the family who had been so good to me, who maybe even thought that I lived a purer life, was an issue to keep procrastinating on in my mind. I wasn't ready to shatter their image of me or maybe even their love for me. Would they still love me? I felt dirty and so unworthy.

As the weeks went on, Samuel and I did talk more, but he was firm that I should have an abortion or choose adoption. I remember sitting in my rolling desk chair with my purple cordless phone pressed to my ear as he told me he had no interest in parenting. "We can't do this. I'm not ready. You're not ready."

My jaw tightened with the realization that my dream of a happy little family wouldn't be happening. My heart sank, and I fumed with anger. How could he give up so easily? How could he not care? How could he not even try? In that moment, the stubbornness dug deeper within me that I would, in fact, carry this baby. I could parent on my own. My mom did, so many others have, and so could I.

I also knew this was the end of my relationship with Samuel forever. If he couldn't be here for me now, or for our baby, he never would be. His true colors had been revealed.

My mom took me to my family doctor to confirm my predicament yet again. My doctor was an Indian lady who looked down at me with stern brown eyes as she pronounced, "You should look into adoption." With tightened lips and internally rolling my eyes, I thought how dare she. This woman I hardly knew beyond giving me prescriptions when I was sick had no right to give input into my personal life. I walked out that door even more determined to keep my baby. I'll show them.

A few days later, my mom then took me to an OBGYN to confirm that my tiny four-foot eleven-inch sixteen-year-old body could even carry a baby to term. It was a valid question and one I'd pondered as well. I remember this doctor being more kind and encouraging, with no judgmental eyes or pushing me toward any decisions.

Oddly, she looked at my feet and said, "What size shoe do you wear?"

"Seven."

"Good. You have a strong foundation, you'll be just fine."

I had always been insecure about my foot size as peers previously had made fun of them in proportion to my small height and skinny legs. Today, though, I was ever so grateful for my larger feet. Being assured that I could carry my baby gave me hope. I later found out that my dad's mom was my height, and she had two nine-pound babies. If she could do it, I could too. Determined to figure all this out, I felt God would help me. I left that office with a package of much-needed information for the newly pregnant, which included backing off on all the typical teenage favorite fried food that I loved.

I'm not sure when Samuel told his parents or how it was done. There wasn't a formal conversation in our living room or a meeting to make plans. Maybe my mom handled that; I don't know. His dad rarely spoke to me even when Samuel and I had been together. He either wasn't there or had been a distant figure without much to say; this situation brought nothing different in that regard. The times I met his mother when he and I were together, she was always friendly and sweet. I knew she felt adoption would be the best choice as well; maybe she mentioned over lunch or perhaps through the voice of Samuel.

Finally, in November, I told my dad and Cyndi over the phone. I had visited at least once while pregnant, but I couldn't find the nerve to bring up the subject and confess. So, a phone call was set up to talk with them. Armed with the knowledge that I needed both of them present for this conversation, Dad and Cyndi were convinced I was either on drugs or pregnant; they had a suspicion that something big was happening in my life. Cyndi told me later that when I shared my news, she slid her back down the wall thinking, "*What are we going to do? How do we support her?*" Her response, though she felt internally in upheaval, was grace-filled: "Thank you for choosing life."

My heart swelled in pride because I felt like in all that I had done wrong... I had done *one* thing right. I was giving this baby life. I could easily have kept this a secret forever; no one would have had to know had I chosen abortion. Yet, I had advocated in the last few weeks for my baby to live. I knew this little baby had a purpose in this world, and I loved the tiny being within me already. The mother bear within me already presented itself, giving me the determination to change my life and do better for this baby. Later they assured me with kindness in their eyes that they hadn't always made good choices growing up, either. My secret shame I had been carrying was met with grace and understanding. *They still loved me!* Looking back years later, I can see that growing up in the midst of Purity Culture I felt my "goodness" was tied to being "pure."

The grace my entire family extended surprised me. My Grandpa, my dad's father, hugged me with the fierceness of a deep love and tears streaming down his face.

"It's okay. God loves you. You will never be too far gone. We love you."

I wasn't being punished or ostracized for my choices as I feared, though natural consequences were playing out; instead, I was embraced through my storm. They poured the fragrance of love and acceptance over me, washing me with forgiveness. It was an example of how Jesus' love, grace, mercy, and forgiveness work, not the condemnation I had prepared for.

My family's response of grace displayed the love of Christ in such a way that the soil of my hardened heart softened, watered by my repentant tears. The seeds of faith planted months before were growing.

CHAPTER 3

Battle of the Heart

I selectively told a few friends that I was pregnant. Ironically, we were reading *The Scarlet Letter* in English class at the same time. I felt much like the main character, Hester Prynne. Even though I hadn't exactly committed adultery, the same shame burning on my chest was very similar. While I wouldn't be forced to wear a letter A sewn on my clothes announcing my sin like Hester, I knew it wouldn't be long before others knew of my sin too as my belly grew. *Would I be an outcast? Judged? Would others continue to shame me beyond the shame I felt myself?*

Little did I know then that just as Hester's letter A meant to be a symbol of shame and eventually symbolizing that she was "able," my situation would eventually become a symbol of a powerful new identity for me, too. God was equipping me to be able as well; I just couldn't see it yet.

Since I was small-framed, it didn't take long for my belly to expand noticeably. Getting ready in the mornings for school, I often slid on a hoodie and jeans tied together with a hair band to hide my belly. Some mornings though, I'd look into the bathroom mirror in an attempt to put on makeup and burst into tears. *Who even are you now?* I felt depressed.

Rejected by Samuel. Weary from the weight of sin and consequences. Some days I couldn't stop crying long enough to face another day and went to sob in my bed instead of going to school.

Morning sickness came full force, and I learned quickly as I dangled over the porcelain bowl dry heaving that I needed to eat food constantly. My mom would make me berry smoothies and pumpkin pancakes to eat on the way to school to tame my stomach. Snacks tucked in my backpack kept me steady during my school days. After school, exhaustion would ripple over me, and I fell into my bed by seven each night. Growing a human was certainly a new way of living. Gone were my night owl tendencies and caring about seemingly meaningless gossip of other high school years. I had responsibilities now, and my body let me know it.

On homecoming night, I tried to step back into normal teenage life, wanting to set aside the stress of my reality for just one weekend. I wanted to feel carefree and silly again in a time when I hardly smiled anymore. Our trio of friends, Melanie, another friend Katie, and I, spent hours decorating sweatshirts in puffy paint with our blue and burgundy school colors and our goofy inside jokes. A boyfriend I had over the summer, Jason, came to town to go with me to the dance, too. While we hadn't meshed well as a couple, he still was a supportive friend and cared for me. We arrived at the football game before the dance, but it wasn't long before my smile slid into a frown. There he was in the stands a few rows away: Samuel.

I hadn't seen him or talked to him in weeks. Panic grabbed me by the throat and squeezed.

"I need to leave. We have to go."

My night was ruined by one glance, one realization that he could go on with life as normal while I carried his baby. He didn't care. I would wear the scarlet letter, though it still was hiding under my shirt at only a few weeks along, while he could pretend as if it never happened. Free of all consequences, or so it seemed to me.

When we arrived home, Jason put his hands on my shoulders and said with concerned frustration in his eyes, "I don't understand the hold he has on you."

He didn't get it, and how could he? He had never been in my shoes. I didn't understand the hold on me either, except that I had created a child with Samuel, and no matter how clear it was that we would never be together, an unspoken bond would always be there. I tucked my anger, hurt, and bitterness down, feeling like I had every right to be upset but wishing I could release it.

As the weeks passed, the pressures of stress and grief were rising, threatening to burst through our 1950s house windows. My mom and I still didn't have a healthy relationship stemming from my childhood. While she was supportive and helpful in many ways, the underlying tension kept elevating between us. We didn't know how to talk about many things well. I'm sure she was grappling with her own grief at my life choices, perhaps even wrestling with her own guilt about how I got into this place. I know she understood what I was facing and didn't want me to struggle as she had when I was born. Still, the yelling and slamming doors increased right along with my morning sickness.

It wasn't the first time mom and I had gone to therapy together, and the musty old building was familiar. We had come here in middle school, too, when the fighting was intense, though I don't remember why we fought then. Gray introduced herself, and I followed her down the hall. She was in her thirties with short black hair and dark-rimmed oval glasses perched on her nose. Walking into Gray's small office, I saw a wall of windows straight ahead, her desk and computer to the left. The environment was serene as an old office could be with plants, pretty pictures, and dimly lit by lamps. I chose the boxy seat under her framed licenses and degrees with a guarded heart, sure that I would be met with judgment and face condemnation of all the things I had done wrong.

Instead, she introduced herself with a soothing and calm voice, unfazed by my situation. Over time, she gained my trust as if she had a key that unlocked the gates of honesty and I felt safe. While Gray certainly was able to be truthful with me as we talked about what decisions lay ahead in my journey and processing emotions, she was always kind and validating.

Quickly she became my ally and my voice in my time of need. She was able to tell all my parents what I had been screaming inside since I was a little girl: I want to live with my dad. She gave me strength and support to lean on when I felt guilty about telling my mom, but I knew this would be the best plan. It wasn't all because of our relationship, though I hoped distance would help; it was also that I needed to get away from the constant reminders of Samuel at school. I needed a fresh start.

It was decided that I would finish the fall semester at my mom's and move to my dad's on Christmas Day. We always traded who I would spend holidays with, and that year I spent both Thanksgiving and Christmas with my mom. This year, though, as my parents met halfway between the two-hour drive I had boxes and bags coming along with me. Grief washed over me again as I set up pictures of friends, my CD collection, and figurines I treasured in my room at my dad's. I felt guilty for how I treated my mom and for hurting her by leaving, yet I had hope that this was the change I needed to step in the right direction.

God made it clear right away that this was where I was meant to be. One of the ladies in the guidance office at my school, Sue Ann, was a sweet, encouraging woman I had grown up with at my dad's church. She even was my babysitter for a time years before, so having a familiar, welcoming, face who loved the Lord was exactly what I needed in my new school. My teacher for my Food and Nutrition elective happened to be another sweet Jesus-loving woman, Ms. Wofford. Her husband and my Pawpaw were best friends, and my dad and stepmom had gone to church with them growing up.

One teacher, Mrs. Dunn, quickly became a compassionate mentor in my life as well. She taught Child Development, fitting for my predicament but also a class I found easy and enjoyable. After class one day, she pulled me aside, and she listened to me as I shared my conflicted heart. She didn't tell me what to do like other adults who had interjected their opinions; instead she was a sounding board and provided encouragement no matter what I decided. She placed a pink construction paper card in my hand, about the size of a postcard. On it she had cut out magazine pictures of flowers blooming out of a watering can and had clipped the words to spell Bloom Where You Are Planted. It listed her phone number on the back with a brief message: "If you ever need a listening ear, I'm here. I know it's hard right now, but you can bloom where you are planted."

That phrase would stick with me for the rest of my life, and I would keep that card displayed as a reminder for years. Yes, my life may get uprooted at times, but I could make something beautiful out of it. God was placing people in my life who reflected Him, surrounding me with the support I needed. It was a solid ground to stand on when I was at my weakest.

My school even had a teen pregnancy support group that would give us an hour out of class each week to connect with others experiencing similar situations and teach us life skills as we prepared for motherhood. It was wonderful to not feel alone, but as the months went by, it became difficult at times when I was the only one even considering adoption. I felt like an outsider at times, even there.

Starting a new school while four months pregnant was difficult but exciting as I looked forward to a new start. I still was able to hide my belly under sweatshirts, but it was growing tighter by the week. Walking the halls with books covering my scarlet letter, I hoped for more time for people to get to know me before judging me. I made acquaintances quickly, and I also had my cousin in the same grade to hang out with, but I missed the closeness of friendships from my old school. My friends at my old school kept in touch through AOL instant messenger, but so much had changed along with the distance, so we began drifting apart.

Within a month, my belly grew to the point that people started asking questions. "Are you pregnant? Who is the dad?" They were curious about all things pregnancy but never judging as I feared. When I found out that my baby was a girl, students in my classes brought her teeny pink outfits as a gift. It was a relief to be surrounded by support, both at home and at school.

Slowly, I was getting my footing in this new normal and became happier. Once morning sickness passed in the second trimester, I enjoyed being pregnant. At eighteen weeks pregnant, sitting at my desk in Child Development class, I felt her kick for the first time– a distinct *thump* to the left of my now flat and stretched belly button. In disbelief and completely unaware of Ms. Dunn's lesson, I placed my hand on that same spot. I prodded my buoyant belly to check if it was indeed her, hoping to get a response. *Thump thump thump.* Though I had seen my baby wiggle on the ultrasound, there was no doubt now: there was a baby alive within me. I treasured each movement of hers like a gift, something special between just the two of us. She could hear the beating of my heart, and I could feel her tiny kicks.

Standing in front of my full-length closet mirror door, I often marveled at my changing body and took pictures of my belly to document her growth. With my tiny waist and short legs, there were exactly zero maternity pants that fit me. I resorted to black yoga pants and stretchy-waisted sweatpants to wear with the maternity shirts I now needed. Fashion and appearances prior to becoming pregnant were something from which I sought pride and value, but being a pregnant teenager forced humility and brought my style down a notch as I was grateful for anything that would fit.

Within my new normal, God had taken away the attention of boys and was chipping away at other obstacles in the way of my soul seeking authentic value and love. More dominos fell, inching me closer and closer to Jesus' feet. Yet as my heart softened, there was still a battle going on within me as well, a raging storm with waves crashing, tossing me to the right and left. *Do I parent this baby? Do I look into adoption?* Logically, adoption made sense; I could admit that, but my heart couldn't bear the thought of leaving her in the arms of another mother and never seeing her again.

I would dare say there was even a battle for my soul itself. My will versus God's will. Giving into worldly desires versus surrendering to God's desires. My soul desperately wanted rest and peace. All I felt was thrashing and unrest as anxiety gripped me. I wanted Jesus to calm the stormy waves engulfing me, but I stubbornly grasped the side of the boat, unwilling to fully trust and take His hand.

In the past, I had heard how God's plans are good and that His ways are not our ways, but I was struggling to believe He could make good of this situation without my input. I was struggling to maintain what little control I had left.

I wanted to parent. *I* wanted to be her mother. I was willing to sacrifice whatever it took to do so, like going to community college instead of moving away, not going to prom or dating, and getting a job to support us. I was willing to walk the straight and narrow. I was bargaining with God: *I'll do anything, just please don't make me let her go.*

Still, a little nudging within my soul whispered differently. *Trust me, for I have good plans for you.*[2] I ignored that gentle whisper within my heart for months and pushed aside talks of adoption. I couldn't even look at the pamphlets about adoption, so I built

_____
2 Read Jeremiah 29:11.

49

walls around my heart protecting me, barricading me and my baby inside no matter the price it would take on our lives or that peace wasn't there. Inside those "protective" walls, I found only terror.

My thoughts were consumed with how I could make it work, and I was grateful that all of my parents were supportive of whatever I decided. They were willing to help me either way. Cyndi was a stay-at-home mom to my brother, sister, and cousins, and she could easily babysit while I finished high school and worked. I would share my room with my daughter, placing a crib in the corner. On school mornings, I would wrap my blue robe around my round belly and make myself cinnamon oatmeal while I looked at Pottery Barn catalogs, dreaming of what her nursery theme would be.

Though my family thought adoption might be best, they didn't pressure me or belittle me into thinking I couldn't parent.

"We support you, Leah. We just want you to make an informed decision, trusting that you know what is best for you."

I met with Gray still even though I had moved two hours away. We made it work whether I traveled to her or she drove to visit with me. I looked forward to our sessions. She was supportive in our counseling sessions as we weighed the pros and cons of each direction, and her guidance kept me stable through processing all my emotions.

My only knowledge of adoption was closed adoption. I had many family members adopted into our family, and I saw that the birth moms who placed them were non-existent. Gone. A figment of our imaginations, never talked about and definitely never seen. I couldn't be that mom to just disappear. I loved her too much to just walk away.

When I found out that she was a girl I named her Kaylee Ann. At the time it wasn't a popular name. I had looked for something unique, and apparently so did the rest of the United States as it flew to one of the top names that year. Kay was for my favorite aunt who had taken me under her wing in a lot of ways, another mother figure in my life. Lee was from my Pawpaw's name (he'd passed away when I was nine) and resembled the "lee" sound in my first name. Ann was Cyndi's middle name and simply sounded right. Each syllable was special to me and a link to our family.

Gleefully I went to the mall to pick out her first outfit, the one in which I envisioned bringing her home from the hospital. Since Kaylee was due in the summer, I picked out a short-sleeved light blush pink outfit. The shirt buttoned up the middle and had two darker pink flowers made out of felt to accent the top. It was simple, but it was adorable to me. Seeing how tiny her newborn outfit was, I couldn't wait to hold her in it. I pictured her tiny arms and legs, her minuscule toes, and I imagined how it would feel to finally snuggle her close. I was ten and thirteen years old when my brother and sister were born. I knew how small they were and the weight of them in my arms. Because of them, I had already learned the basics like how to hold a newborn's head properly, soothe a crying baby, and change a diaper. I felt confident I could do that for Kaylee, too.

However, as the gentle nudges continued in my soul and my parents encouraged me to make an informed decision, I finally decided to look for birth moms and teen moms to talk to. I figured that there would be no better people to ask what both paths were like than those walking it themselves. Back then, social media wasn't a thing yet, but there were website forums. Typing in the search bar for my request, I found Hotmail groups to join. Quickly I introduced myself and began asking questions and reading their stories. It was within those groups that I not only made some of my most supportive long-distance friendships but also where my eyes were opened to the hard realities of teen motherhood and to things I hadn't considered. My stubborn resolve to parent was beginning to fade. *Was I really ready for this? Was this the life I really wanted for her?*

One group was called "Adoptions of Love," and it happened to be filled with many Jesus followers. Again, God was providing the solid support I needed and placing people in my path from all over the country. There were birth moms and adoptive moms in there who had incredible relationships surrounding their children with love at the center. Their stories showed love and appreciation for all sides of the adoption triad: adoptive parent, birth parent, and adoptee. There were two adoptive moms in particular who each had open adoptions with their child's birth mothers and it encouraged me to see that adoptive moms could extend and open their hearts to birth moms as well. They each spoke highly of the birth mom in their life, considering them friends, and often sharing pictures from recent visits. These adopted mothers wanted birth mothers in their lives and cherished the presence these women had. It was clear the adoptive moms weren't threatened by having a birth mother in their lives. I was surprised and amazed to see that this type of relationship was even possible!

It was in that group that I also met Breanna, who would become a best friend and confidant despite being states away. She was two years older than me, and at the time, it had been about six months since she'd placed her daughter in an open adoption. We had uncanny similarities from both loving pot roast as our favorite home-cooked comfort food to the biological father of our children having the same name. Her story reflected a similar experience to the adoptive mothers in the group, one marked with friendship and openness. She shared that as soon as she knew adoption was the choice for her early in pregnancy, she was able to pick the future adoptive parents and started their relationship even months before birth. It was relieving to hear from someone else who had walked this path and to have someone tell me what it actually was like to choose adoption, but most of all, to find a friend who understood the battle I was feeling inside.

I had no idea open adoption was a thing. My agency had never conducted one before due to the laws in North Carolina at the time, so it wasn't presented as an option. Semi-open adoption or closed was most common back then, but I knew that even letters and pictures wouldn't be enough to help me move forward in life and for Kaylee to know how much I love her. There's only so much that can be expressed in written words and posing for photos. I desperately wanted a relationship with her, so in my mind at the time, that meant parenting was the only option for me.

Learning about open adoption gave me a new perspective. The realization that this kind of relationship was possible began tumbling down the walls I had built protecting my wishes and desires. It was beginning to feel like there actually could be a middle-ground option that would be the best of both worlds, one where I could grow up myself but also still watch her grow. One where she knew how much I loved her and where she could know me, too. One where I could be there for milestones and visit with her.

This new information was opening my eyes, but I still was grasping to control the narrative I wanted for our life. I wasn't ready to choose adoption. At night, more times than I could count, I would have recurring dreams that Samuel would show up at my high school unexpectedly and kiss me. If he'd just come back, I thought it would all be okay. If he'd just come back, maybe I would be able to parent her. I was still so angry with him. The hurt, rejection, and bitterness I kept tucked down were bubbling to the surface, adding to the battle within me. I wanted answers. I wanted reconciliation. I wanted to find peace, and I thought the only way to do that meant finding peace with him.

Turns out, I was still looking to the wrong person to save me from the mess I was in.

Part 2

THE CHOICE
AND THE PEACE

Oh little girl,
if only you knew
the love surrounding you.
Looking at you I see
what God intended this to be
An amazing journey of
love for one little girl
who has changed so many worlds

I pray others will see
all the wonderful people
in your life there are
and always will be.

-Leah, Spring 2005

CHAPTER 4

View from the Mountain Top

After moving in with my dad, my relationship with my mom did improve drastically as I had hoped. The distance was exactly what we needed to set aside daily living stressors and focus on our relationship. I would visit on some weekends, just like before when I would meet my dad but now in reverse. They still met halfway to trade off time for many months as I still didn't have my driver's license. After I got my driving permit, we used these trips to practice driving on the highway with a parent in the car to guide me.

One April Sunday while visiting, my Mom and I decided to take an easy hike to enjoy the beautiful weather before I went back home. Pilot Mountain was relatively nearby, and we had gone many times in previous years. She let me drive my stepbrother's old white Mazda to practice more driving. Spiraling up the mountain road, up and up, we finally reached the top parking lot. The newly spring air still had a slight chill to it that mid-morning. My basketball-like seventh-month belly was protruding under an old dance team t-shirt, and a light jacket kept me warm. Yoga pants still were all that fit me, which was perfect for the walk ahead.

We had a picnic lunch of sandwiches to fill up my always hungry stomach before we started our small hike. I don't remember our conversations, but I remember it being a good day and enjoying time with my mom. The Carolina blue sky and fresh air were as refreshing as this healing mother-daughter relationship.

Pilot Mountain has several short loops of rewarding trails to explore that are less than a mile long. We reached the lookout point, my hands resting in my jacket pockets as I admired the view of the distinguishable knob jutting across the small valley. Around the knob most of the area was flat and I could see for miles to nearby cities and other mountain ranges that peaked out of the earth. I had seen this same view multiple times before, and it honestly wasn't as breathtaking as the Blue Ridge mountains I was born in, but it fascinated me to see a bird's-eye view of the world below.

That day, though, something was different. That day it was even more beautiful and breathtaking as the seed of grace blossomed in my soul. The sunshine seeped right down through the cracks formed as my hardened heart had been softening over the last few months.

As my hair danced in the breeze, I felt God there with me, like a warm presence that whispered in my ear and straight to my soul. *See this view? Just as there is more to see from this perspective above, so I can see the big picture for your life. Trust me.*[3]

As if a veil were lifted from my eyes, I saw our reality clearer than ever. No longer was it hazy

---

3 Read Isaiah 55:8–9.

through my naive eyes, certain that I could be a supermom and expect my daughter to turn out any different than me. I finally saw the truth.

I saw how Kaylee's life would look: filled with babysitters and a single mom constantly working towards an education or working to pay the bills, just like my mom. I saw a little girl wondering why her father didn't want to be around, which felt even worse than what I'd had growing up. At least I had my dad every other weekend. I saw myself desperately wishing I could provide nicer things for her than I could afford. I saw us struggling. It hurt deeply to look within myself and see my many shortcomings, not just physically and financially, but emotionally. As much as I desperately wanted to be everything she needed, I wasn't mature enough yet to be the kind of mom I wanted to be. Like eyes adjusting to bright light after being in the dark, it was painful to peek into our future and the life I had to offer Kaylee.

The ugliness I saw when God unveiled my heart anguished me deeply, and I sobbed the rest of the day. The weight of my sin and choices was so heavy that I think I cried mostly to cleanse myself of it all. I cried for the choices I had made in the past. I cried for the choice I had to make for our future. I grieved with an ugly, blotchy-faced, snot-filled cry. I kept crying as my mom drove me to meet my dad. I think I tried to explain what I felt as we waited for my dad, but I needed more time to really process. Tears kept streaming as my dad drove me home.

"Are you okay? Did something happen?" he asked, but all I could do was shake my head and cry more.

We sat there in silence, my dad unsure of how to comfort me, and honestly nothing could comfort me in that moment as I mourned.

Hours later my tears dried up, and I took a cleansing breath as I cried out to Jesus. *Please God, what do you want me to do? Take this pain away. Show me what to do. My way isn't working.*

Now alone in my room, the final domino had fallen, and I had reached the end of myself. The dominos that had raced forward tipping one decision into the next had finally caught up with me, crashing me face down at His feet. *Trust me, child. Trust me with your life and Kaylee's. I've got you. I've got it all worked out. Just trust me.*[4]

This time I was finally ready to take His hand and stand upright once more. I surrendered my heart to God. I surrendered my desire to parent my baby girl, who was kicking happily in my belly unknowing of the turmoil in my heart just outside my womb. Much like a child giving up her stubborn tantrum and yielding to her wise parent, I yielded my everything, laid it down at His feet, finally realizing He knew what was best for me. With a deep breath and the peace that encompassed me, I felt a new strength for what He was calling me to do. Adoption.

For the first time in many months— maybe years, maybe ever— the weight in my soul lifted,

---

4 Read Proverbs 3:5–6.

and I knew what I had to do. It was a supernatural hug from my Heavenly Father, saying that He had plans to prosper me, not to harm me.[5] It was a gentle reminder that He loves me and forgives me. It was a loving embrace in which I felt Him there with me in a more real way than ever before. I now knew without a doubt that I was a child of God. Ransomed. Redeemed. Forgiven. Loved. With that peace, I realized He was my strength for what He was calling me to do.

Sharing with my parents how the Lord had worked on my heart, they gave their support and encouragement again that this was my choice and that they would be here with me no matter what. "I'm ready to look at profile books." My voice trembled as I relayed my decision to Gray. While I was certain this was the right step, I still felt nervous about this unknown path less traveled, and I questioned what it would entail for me to personally walk upon it. *Will it turn out like Breanna's open adoption? What if I lose contact with Kaylee forever?* Questions and fears rolled through my mind, things I couldn't answer that tempted me to yank back control. It was a risk I was taking to trust another family to uphold their promises for the relationship I desperately wanted.

CHOOSING HER FAMILY

The following week, Gray and I talked about what I desired in a family for my little girl. My family

5 Jeremiah 29:11

shared their thoughts with me, and we worked together on a list of ideals. It helped to think through all the ways that, if I could be the mom that I wished I could be for her right now, what would that look like? And, if I had an ideal open adoption as Breanna's, what would that look like? Part of my list stemmed from my own childhood and what I found helpful or wished I had.

My basic list to narrow down profiles included:

- A Christian family who genuinely loved the Lord
- Lived within the same state, or close to borders in neighboring states, so visiting would be easy
- Had a child already, whether through adoption or biologically. Since I was a lonely only child most of my years growing up, I wanted to guarantee she would have a sibling to play with
- Extended family nearby as a support system as I had seen the value of this at my dad's house
- A stay-at-home mom, or flexible jobs to be with Kaylee as often as possible
- Most importantly, desired an open adoption relationship with visits

Finding a family that would be authentically honest and who shared the same vision of open adoption was my top priority. While I kept putting one foot in front of the other with peace as my compass, I kept praying to the One who was holding my hand through this process, assuring me to trust Him. I trusted that He knew the right family for her and one that would love me, too.

Within another week, Gray had collected family profiles to look through. She had driven to my dad's house to have a counseling meeting with my dad, stepmom, and I, and then she would drive me the two hours to my mom's house in the company car for our weekend visit. It was in that company car as trees passed by in a blur that three profiles sat in my lap. We chose this two-hour ride to have space and time for just the two of us to think and talk through them.

"Start with these three books, and if you don't find anything you connect with, I have more in the backseat."

I glanced at the backseat as she spoke; there were stacks of them just as she said. As she drove down the highway, my heartbeat quickened, and my hands shook. *Was I actually doing this? Would I find good people to love her and me well? Are there actually families who will keep their promises and want an open adoption? Lord, guide me. Show me the ones.*

Back then, profile books were done differently. There weren't fancy photo book options and custom services to help create books like there are today. Two of the profiles sitting on my lap were large scrapbooks. When I looked through them later, it was clear that hours of work had been put into them by hand to make them beautiful. The profile on top stood out. It was simple: a folded up typed letter to me and a small photo flip book. "This family just has been approved to adopt and didn't have time to make a scrapbook, but they wanted to present to you," Gray informed me as I eyed the top profile.

Taking a deep breath of resolve, I ran my finger over the cover's edge and flipped open a four-by-six photo book with plastic insert pages. I wanted to see what this family looked like before I read what they had to say to me in their letter, putting faces with their names. The first photo made me draw in a quick breath– it was as if I was looking at my own family photo from the 1990s. In the picture was the dad, the mom, their three-year-old son, and their dog posed in front of the Christmas tree. The mom, Christine, with her long brown hair reminded me of my stepmom when she was in her twenties. The dad, Phillip, had brown hair like my dad. Their son, Blake, had bright blonde hair like I did as a child. Their dog looked exactly like the dog I had grown up with at my dad's house: a red short-haired dachshund. Immediately peace filled my soul, fueling me to keep turning those pages to discover what other similarities and clues I could find that these might be the ones.

Turning each page, I felt God's warm comfort with me. In each photo, I was introduced to extended family members, the fun things they did as a family, and their home, giving me a glimpse into the life my daughter could have. Each photo radiated love. Though I still had many questions to ask them to be sure we would be on the same page, I felt encouraged and hopeful. I felt at peace. *Maybe these are the ones.*

Unfolding two typed pages, I then read their letter to me. Each paragraph described their physical appearance, hobbies, their involvement within the church, personalities, and how much they enjoyed their son. They seemed like a wonderful family, but it was the second page that spoke to my heart. It spoke of how close they are with their siblings and how they wanted that for their son, too, just like I wanted that for Kaylee. Most of all, their words penned to me were marked with kindness and compassion:

> *"From watching our friends and family, we know going through pregnancy and birth is not an easy thing to do, physically or emotionally. We also understand that with the added decisions you are facing, the stress must be overwhelming. We would be happy to meet with you if you wish and to help you in any way we can.*
>
> *Thank you from the bottom of our hearts for giving a couple like us the opportunity to be a mommy and daddy. May God richly bless you and this child all the days of your lives, and may He give you wisdom and peace in this time of decision.*

*We know you will make the best
choice for you and your baby."*

Their written blessings floated into my soul
as I read. Their words made me feel seen, not just
because of the baby I was carrying but because they
loved a God Who loved me, too. They were praying for
blessings, wisdom, and peace over *me* and my baby.
My heart was encouraged, bringing more clarity by
the minute to God's plan.

As I read through the other two family profiles,
there weren't the same similarities or feelings
evoked from them I had with Christine and Phil's.
Still, I decided to set aside the last scrapbook as a
backup. Over the rest of the ride, I shared with Gray
what I was thinking and gravitating towards. With a
new ease and openness towards taking another step
towards adoption, I relayed, "I want to meet Christine
and Phil, and if that doesn't feel right, then I will meet
with the second family." The lightness of my heart
assured me that I was still on the right path as we
met my mom in the agency parking lot and I shared
my plan with her.

My mom and I spent the weekend together,
talking more about the family that might be the
ones. Mom was supportive, but I could detect a hint
of sadness and even some concern in the questions
she had. I realized this choice of adoption was going
to affect more than just me; it would grieve many
members of my family as well.

Over the following week, we prepared to meet Christine and Phil. My parents and I discussed the fears we had and questions to consider. We felt optimistic, but still, they encouraged me to take my time and make sure this was what I wanted to do. Being nearly eight months pregnant, though, I could feel the moments of time slipping past quickly. I needed to make a decision, and I wanted to have time to build a relationship with whatever family I chose.

Tearing out a sheet of notebook paper, I wrote in my bubbly handwriting a few things I wanted to know about them and their lifestyle:

- How often do they work?
- Will they take time off work after she comes?
- How did they meet?
- How long have they been married?
- Is extended family in the area?
- Are they willing to let us come to milestones and events?
- What does their vision of open adoption look like?
- How do they discipline?
- What is their church denomination, and how involved are they?
- What do they do for fun with Blake?

Ready as I could be for our meeting, we climbed into our dated Dodge white van and made the two hour trip to the agency's office. The Carolina weather was climbing into the summer-like heat portion of spring as the days inched closer to May. A dusty rose short-sleeved maternity shirt covered my watermelon-shaped belly, paired with my typical black yoga pants and new black platform sandals. The nerves rolled within me right along with the tires on the pavement under us. *Would they like me? What if I don't know what to talk about? What if I don't feel like we connect; what then?*

We had arrived first, and I was grateful for the time to get settled and talk with Gray for a few minutes to make a discussion plan. Our meeting room was set up with a couch under a window with another couch facing it, along with other chairs brought in along the sides for everyone to have a seat. Plopping down on the left side of the couch under the window, I took off my flip-flop sandals and immediately put my legs up in criss-cross applesauce style to get comfortable after the long ride. My mom, stepdad, dad, Cyndi, and Gray were there as my support, and they assured me that if the conversation lulled, they would help fill in with questions. I eyed the door nervously as I waited for them to come in.

And then they did, filing in after one another, including three-year-old Blake, whom I had asked to meet as well. I was taken back at how tall Christine was, being quite the opposite of little me. The room filled with awkward smiles and courteous "hello's" but it was Blake who quickly came to the rescue with comic relief. Immediately he spotted my flip-flops below me and tried them on. Parading around the room in massive shoes compared to his tiny feet was hilarious. He unknowingly broke through the nervousness for us as we laughed together.

"He loves shoes," they told us. I giggled and assured them it was okay that he borrowed them.

Having a laugh helped the room to settle into conversation easier, and it was truly an easy conversation. Phil was charismatic and funny, while Christine was quiet and thoughtful, and I instantly felt comfortable with them. As I asked my questions, I kept a check on my feelings. I sensed honesty in their answers. We talked about how they parent Blake and what their daily life is like. They talked about their close family and how important that was to them. They shared about their jobs and their plans for taking time off. When I asked how they met and how they knew they were the ones for each other, Phil told the sweetest story of knowing she was different when she asked for something other than pepperoni on her pizza like everyone else. I could sense the love they had for one another and how hard they were working to create a life guided by God.

After getting to know each other more, we dove into the open adoption conversation. *Would they be willing? Did we have the same vision of what open adoption meant to me?* They shared with me how Blake was also adopted, and while they had some contact and visits with his birth mom, not having a way to reach her often weighed on their hearts.

"When I'm so excited that he's done something new, I wish that I could share it with her, too, but I can't," Christine said with sincerity in her voice, "That's why we hope to have more contact with you to share more moments."

Their experience with a semi-open adoption prepped their hearts for the very same vision of the fully open adoption I desired.

"We believe that you are an important piece to her life puzzle. We want you here to help fill in the pieces that we can't," assured Phil.

His statement stood out to me then, like a sticky note with an inspirational quote attached to my bathroom mirror, and it remains today the foundation of our agreement.

I shared my hopes of visiting at least twice a year, once in the summer around her birthday and in December around Christmas. While no one can predict exactly what they will feel when actually walking through the adoption journey emotions, I felt that was a conservative minimum amount and what my heart could handle between visits. I knew I would miss Kaylee deeply. I knew I would want to see her and how she's grown, but I didn't want to ask too much. Two visits felt like a happy medium that was doable for both families. and if more visits could happen naturally, then that would be great!

The peace of the Lord was tangible as if He were physically sitting on the couch beside me. My confidence grew with each topic discussed that they would raise her in ways that I wished that I could at sixteen years old. I began to trust them to invite me into their hearts alongside my daughter, and honor our agreement. I can't say that I made my decision to pick them right there in that room as I still went home to ponder and pray, but much like the feeling of discovering your soul mate, I had a deep knowing: *This is it. This is the family.*

GOD SIZED FINGERPRINTS

"Leah, Gray is on the phone for you," my stepmom called out. I answered on our home's cordless phone timidly wondering what she needed to talk about.

"I talked with Christine and Phil about keeping Kaylee Ann's name. You'll never believe this."

I panicked a little. They felt like the perfect family, but what if they didn't want to keep her name? What would I do then?

I braced myself for rejection as she continued, "They had already picked out a name but quickly agreed to the name you had picked right away. Get this— Their name was *Kayla* Ann. They love the name you picked and think it's perfect!"

Awe and relief washed over me. I was so grateful for their agreement in this detail, and I still am. It was another fingerprint of God to show me the way, confirmation yet again to trust Him and follow His lead. He was making it clear that He heard my prayers and that He was trustworthy in every little detail.

You see, a name isn't just a name. It holds pieces of culture, identity, family roots, and meanings. Especially for adoptees, names carry the weight of many important connections. Keeping her name Kaylee Ann meant in my eyes that my place mattered to them, that the name I had spoken over her while in my womb for months mattered. And to Kaylee, 19 years old at the writing of this book, it means a beautiful combination of both her adoptive and biological sides, each syllable's significance intermingled with family members on all sides. It's always been her name, and it's always been honored.

Another beautiful gesture that assured my heart of their character was that they agreed to create and sign an open adoption agreement. Now, back in 2004, this was completely unheard of. Would it have held up in court as the first open adoption of our agency if needed? Probably not. But, our word was our bond. It was a document that we could go back to if something went off course, words written in irrefutable black and white. We promised simple things as a bare minimum, and it settled my heart.

- We would have at least two visits a year
- In between visits, we would communicate with updates and photos
- If we ever moved or changed our phone number, we would notify the other with the new information so we couldn't just disappear

We agreed to these terms, typed it up, and had our signatures notarized. Along with the notary seal stamped on that paper was the seal on my heart, the seal of a promise that I was trusting them to uphold.

The Lord's view from the mountain top— the big picture He was revealing to us one detail at a time— was becoming more beautiful than I ever imagined. Yet, even with peace as my harness and glimpses of His big picture along the way, the climb to see the view at the mountaintop in this season of life was not easy.

CHAPTER 5

Last Days As Mine

Cyndi casually stood facing me, with her back leaning against the oven handle as she did so often, excitement beamed in her eyes.

"Leah, dad and I were talking and...we thought it might be helpful for you to have something to love on and nurture if you do choose adoption. To help with the grief."

Glancing back and forth between my dad's eyes and Cyndi's, I waited expectantly for her to explain.

"So, we were wondering what you thought about getting *puppies*? We found dachshunds that need a home. We know they can never replace Kaylee, but we want to do all we can to help you through this."

Gleefully surprised and touched by the efforts they were willing to go in support of me, I hugged them as best as I could with my belly in the way. Of course, I agreed that puppies would be wonderful! A few days later, we went with my siblings to meet the litter and their mother at the farm. One was the runt of the litter, and I immediately felt a connection to her. She was small, just like me.

We brought them home a few weeks later in May. I had named my puppy Chloe, and my brother—

6 years old at the time— named her sister Chasey because she ran around the farm chasing him. Both had black, short fur with brown around their noses and paws. Chasey was bigger than Chloe and always would be, and I loved that.

On the long drive home, Chloe kept whimpering, so I picked her up to comfort her. She quickly nestled against the roundness of my belly and fell asleep in my lap. I felt such joy to have chosen her and for her to have chosen me in return. Now, I see the irony that I was separating her from her mother for my comfort as I prepared to be separated from my daughter.

However, it was honestly the most perfect timing as my eighth month of pregnancy was weighing on me both physically and emotionally. Our new puppies were a consolation prize for what was coming ahead in my grief. While puppies could never replace the child I would be placing into another family's arms, they served as a coping tool along with my counseling, support groups online, and my family around me. In fact, within my birth mother groups, pets are a common solution to help with the healing process. It's proven in studies that pets can actually be more comforting than humans![6] No wonder therapy dogs and other pets exist.

6 Bobak, Ashley. " Pets More Effective for Grief Support than Humans, Study Finds." Mad in America. June 22, 2021. https://www.madinamerica.com/2021/06/pets-effective-grief-support-humans-study-finds/

I'm grateful my parents leaned into their intuition of what might help me through my grief, which had already begun. I often sat uncomfortably crisis-crossed on the floor of my dad's living room cuddling my new puppy with a heaviness inside. Barely the size of my forearm, she fit perfectly into my cradled arm and into the aching crevices of my heart.

THE END OF JUNIOR YEAR

I remained in school as long as I could, but I was reaching my breaking point. One day I was sitting in Spanish class, and I just could not find a comfortable position. I wiggled, ached, moved, and winced. Sitting in hard seats for most of my day was becoming an issue, along with fitting my now extra-large belly behind a desk. My school had been incredibly accommodating; I even had been given special permission to be late for class since I had to waddle my way from one side of the school to the other and needed frequent bathroom stops. However, one day as I waddled to my Algebra 2 class, a stern teacher who didn't know this arrangement called me out in the hallway while I was walking alone. "What are you still doing in the hallways?! Where is your hall pass?" I immediately broke down crying, unable to control the tidal wave of hormones, discomfort, and emotions rolling out of me. Her chastising broke the dam of my resolve.

As I stood there sobbing, unable to speak up for myself while this teacher stared dumbfounded, the Lord sent Ms. Dunn down the hallway at just the right time. She said, "I'll take it from here. She's one of my students."

"What happened, Leah?" she asked me once we were alone.

I cried until I found the words of how uncomfortable I was, the sensitivity felt by the unjust hall pass issue, and I just wanted to go home. Calling my stepmom for me, she advocated for me to do just that. This turn of events forced us to reconsider schooling options. We discussed the pros and cons of finishing the year from home. With just a few weeks left of both the school year and my pregnancy, that was my vote. I needed a doctor's approval, however, to medically excuse me from my school and have my work sent home. At my next weekly OBGYN appointment, Cyndi and I presented our case for why this was best for me and advocated for that.

My doctor looked at me and said, "Promise me you'll graduate. Promise me this is just to finish the year and then you'll go back."

I agreed. Yes, absolutely! I wanted that, too. I wanted this baby to be proud of me one day, knowing that I didn't waste the second chance offered me. With my doctor's note in hand, I was beyond grateful to be able to finish comfortably at home while still making good grades. A year later when I graduated high school, I sent my graduation announcement to the OBGYN office to show that I held true to my promise.

One morning while doing schoolwork, I got a phone call from my neighbor, Angie, across the street who had kids the same ages as my siblings. "Leah, Jensen forgot her lunch box. Could you come grab it so that Cyndi can take it to school with her?"

"Sure, be right over," I agreed while anxiety began beating in my chest.

While our families were close, I had never been in her house before. She usually came here to visit with Cyndi. Crossing the street, I knocked on the side door I'd seen others use.

Angie ushered me in, "It's right in there," pointing to the dining room's swinging door.

I opened it, and...

"SURPRISE!" the room shouted. Cyndi, my Nanny, my aunt, and more of Cyndi's supportive friends beamed at me, excited that they managed the surprise.

And what did I do? I burst into tears, as usual. I was so caught off guard, so overwhelmed by their love for me. I was also confused. Why are they here? What are we celebrating? It wasn't my birthday.

Cyndi rushed to hug me as I cried on her shoulder. "Sweetheart," I am always her sweetheart and my dad is her honey. "We wanted to throw you a Leah shower. We know you won't have a baby shower, but we felt it was only fair to still love on you and shower you simply for being you. We love you!"

After my emotions calmed, we ate snacks they had lovingly prepared, always a favorite thing to do during pregnancy. We moved our small party to the living room where they had each brought gifts for me. There weren't baby onesies and bottles; instead, there were things for me. Gift cards to the mall to buy new clothes that fit after the baby was born. Spa gift cards and lotions to pamper myself. Devotionals and other books to lean into my newfound faith as I navigated my grief and became a new version of me. And, my favorite, I received tons of scrapbooking supplies to document my story and pictures of Kaylee as she grew.

Looking around the room, my heart brimmed with joy. In awe that I had so many people supporting me and doing everything possible to help me not to feel forgotten even though I wasn't parenting, my tears were good tears this time. While prepping for a baby's birth typically is a joyful occasion, I was prepping for loss. Yet, these special women took time to make sure I still had my moment as any new mother should— even if it looked a bit different.

PREPARING FOR BIRTH & LOSS

June 3rd, 2004, Gray arrived at my dad's house for a counseling session with a folder in hand. Settling in on the green, burgundy, and gold plaid living room couch, she checked in on how I was feeling emotionally and about my decision of adoption. She validated my feelings with her calming voice like she always did as we chatted about school ending well and my increased emotions, now being thirty-eight weeks pregnant. Even with my common weepy moments and apprehension of what was coming, I still was feeling at peace in my decision. To an outsider who hasn't experienced the peace of Christ, it seems unnatural. Adoption also *is* unnatural. It is the separation of a biological mother from her child, and in an ideal world—a sinless world—it wouldn't be needed at all. Yet supernatural peace continued to strengthen me, carrying me moment by moment towards the redemption of our story.

Still, we discussed coping tactics for grief, both for now and after birth. Even with a supernatural peace that this was the right decision for us, the grieving process was still a reality. She encouraged me to keep getting my feelings out in healthy ways and to not stuff them down.

"Think of a soda bottle. If you keep shaking it up, eventually it will explode from the pressure. But, if you let a little bit of the air out at a time by slowly releasing the lid, it doesn't explode everywhere. That's what grief needs, too. Let it out a little at a time. Every time a feeling comes up, let it out. Talk about it, write about it, draw about it. Do something with it, but don't let it build up so that it explodes."

That concept made perfect sense to me and is something I held onto, something I still do to this day. Writing and prayer became my biggest pressure release, often at the same time in a prayer journal. I had also already been blogging for months to capture memories and feelings surrounding this experience for only a few private friends to see, and it helped to share my feelings. My Adoptions of Love online support group also was a treasured place to ask questions and share feelings with others who understood the complexities of what I was walking through.

Moving onto the next topic, she gazed at me with soft care in her eyes and said, "I wanted to let you know that Samuel has already signed the papers to terminate his rights." I felt both relief that he wouldn't contest the adoption plan that I felt was best for Kaylee and sadness that this was another reminder of how easily his life had moved on. With that, she opened up her manila file folder and pulled out paperwork to prep for my hospital plan. These weren't physical preferences like whether I wanted an epidural or not, but preferences sensitive to the adoption experience I desired in the hospital. Working through each question, we discussed options and thought through what I envisioned for support during labor and the first days of her life. Our last days together before she would head home in one direction, and I would go to my home in another.

- *Do I want the adoptive family to visit me?* Yes.
- *Do I want them in the delivery room?* No, I want my mom and stepmom.
- *Do I want to hold the baby and keep her in my room?* Yes, absolutely!

- *Do I want newborn pictures taken?* Of course!
- *Do I want a copy of the original birth certificate and footprints?* Without a doubt.
- *Am I comfortable staying on the mother/baby floor after delivery?* Yes.
- *Do I want any visitors?* Yes, if I feel up to it.
- *Do I want to breastfeed while in the hospital?* Yes, because I know it is beneficial, but I was also unsure if it would make emotions harder.

Everyone around me reminded me that while we can make plans, sometimes we don't know how we will feel when we are in the moment.

At the bottom of the hospital plan form, Gray typed, "Leah has spent a lot of time carefully considering an adoption plan and hopes that her wishes will be respected. If she changes her mind concerning any of the above, this, too should be respected." I loved her advocacy for *me*. Feeling like she had my back no matter what, along with my family, was helping me to feel a little more ready for the hospital whenever Kaylee decided to make her arrival.

Answering each hospital question cemented the reality that, ready or not, my baby was coming within weeks, and my time was ticking away. There was absolutely nothing I could do about it, even if I chose to parent, these were our last days with her being just mine within me. Soon, I would be sharing her. Pregnancy is a bit of a paradox in that it feels like you'll be pregnant forever, yet it also only seems to last for a blink. Wanting time to speed up yet also slow down was quite a conundrum. It was all too much and not enough at the same time.

The following days, I continued to write in my journal and talk to my friends online. Having birth moms to talk with who had experienced what I was about to go through was an immense help in preparing. They understood the giant, looming question marks of what birth would be like and how I would handle the tidal wave of emotions threatening to crash any day. I prepared for the worst and hoped for the best.

With not even a false alarm to report, I felt growing frustration and wondered if labor would *ever* come. Surely, I would be pregnant forever. It felt that way. The other teen moms in my school had given birth to their babies. I was the last. Even in my online communities, it felt like I was the last. Cyndi encouraged me to "nest" and be more physically active with some chores at home and by taking walks around the mall together. Finally, my doctor agreed to induce me on my due date, June 11th. I mostly wanted this option to make sure that everyone who was traveling to support me had a heads up. My mom, Kaylee's new parents, my social worker, and even my newfound online birth mom friend, Breanna, were driving to be by my side. I *needed* my support system in place, and my doctor agreed.

Knowing that June 11th would be her birthday if all went as planned, I hunkered down to prepare emotionally for the storm ahead and treasured every last kick and roll. I decided I wanted to write Kaylee a letter, so even if we lost touch, she had this from me. She would know why I chose adoption, what I envision for her life, my thoughts, and most importantly my love for her.

Saturday June 5th, 2004

My baby girl Kaylee Ann,

I don't know where to start except to say I love you. I want you to always know and remember you are loved! I love you with all my heart, and I haven't even really met you yet.

As I'm writing this, you are still in my tummy. I love feeling you move. I love every doctor's visit. That's how I know you are growing well and healthy. I pray that you never think that I didn't want you. That is far from the truth. I've wanted to be your mommy from the beginning, but being so young myself, I know you deserve a better life. This choice has been the hardest decision I've ever had to make. I know in my heart and mind it is what's best. I know you will have a wonderful life with the family I've chosen for you. Through an open adoption you not only have your adoptive family, but your birth family as well to love you! You are surrounded by love!

Know that I love you and will always be here for you. You are so special to me. A gift from God. You've changed my life for the better. Your arrival has made me a stronger, better person, and I thank God everyday for you and my experiences.

I keep reading this over and over hoping I've included everything I want to say. But I guess the truth is, this letter can only begin to explain how much I love you and how blessed you are. Our story is just beginning. Our story and love will go on forever. This letter just marks the beginning of it! I look forward to visits, pictures, emails, and watching you grow. I will treasure this time I've had with you forever.

Love,
Leah (your birth mommy)

THE LAST DAY AS ONLY MINE

In my mind, I narrated every seemingly normal thing that I did on our last full day together before Kaylee arrived. *This is my last breakfast with her within me. My last time getting ready with her. My last day of her being all mine.* No moment went wasted; it was all acknowledged and honored. I'm still like this today as we have our firsts together. Nothing is too small to be acknowledged as important in my time with her.

My little brother's seventh birthday was June 8th, but my parents decided to hold off on his party until June 10th so that Christine and Phil could meet a lot of our extended family, and vice versa. I felt excited for them to arrive, relieved they were nearby and ready to meet our daughter as much as I was.

I was physically ready as well. My extremely large watermelon waist was heavy to lug around, and I was over it. My once baggy maternity shirts now barely fit over my belly. Christine and Phil arrived with Blake, and he immediately asked in his adorably curious voice, "Did you swallow a watermelon?!" We all laughed at his innocent question, explaining there was a baby in my belly.

We gathered at a local community pool for Andrew's party, watching the kids splash in the water while the adults— and me, who fit in more with the adults— sat around tables chatting. I don't remember the conversations, but I remember the feeling of looking around and feeling content.

There was joy that my family, both my own and the family I'd chosen for my daughter, were together. Aunts, uncles, cousins, and grandparents came to celebrate– and even my mom was there. She had arrived to be by my side throughout Kaylee's birth. I have always admired that I can have *all* my family together; despite any differences, my parents set those aside because of their love for me. While we were gathering for my brother, they also were there for me. I loved watching everyone talk with Christine and Phil and watching my siblings play with Blake. They were immersed in my family, and it felt natural. As the sky dimmed, we said our goodbyes and prepared for our early morning hospital arrival.

Of course, I couldn't sleep well out of excitement and nerves, so I eased slowly into the desk chair with my nightly snack of cereal in a bag, ready to log into AIM (AOL instant messenger) to talk with my friends from all places. That was the beauty of the growing internet at the time; I felt so connected to people I had not yet met in person. They knew tomorrow was the big day, and I had many people checking in on me and cheering me on. With dings every few seconds I clicked back and forth between the little boxes that held our conversations.

Terri, the leader of the Adoptions of Love group, sent a message that helped me to pause and refocus my heart on the Lord. In all my excitement that tomorrow was finally going to be the big day, I needed this reminder.

TLynnP9: how are you doing emotionally?

lele87: doing good actually. I thought I'd be going crazy, but I'm actually really calm

TLynnP9: That's good to hear, but prepare yourself sweetie, after tomorrow you are going to have so many emotions going on within you. Just remember... God is with you at all times and He will be the one to give you strength. Keep praying to Him. He will be the one to guide you through this, because He is the one who brought you on this journey and He is guiding you as His servant be blessed much by His grace.

lele87: I'll definitely remember that, thank you

TLynnP9: Can I pray for you?

lele87: that would be great

TlynnP9: Heavenly Father, thank you for all that you do and continue to do in our lives. I ask that you be with Leah and continue to guide her and continue to give her strength *when she feels weak. Let Leah have a smooth and easy delivery and a healthy baby girl. She is following you, Lord. Kaylee is so blessed to have Leah, Christine, and Phil. I ask that you be with them all tomorrow and let them share in so many memories and cherish each and every memory of this special day. Lord, we thank you for bringing them all together and showing them the amount of love a child can have. We thank you Father for the journey of motherhood and the birth of Kaylee. We ask this Father in your name. Amen.*

lele87: *that was beautiful, Terri. Thank you.*

Her words, though only typed, ushered in the presence of God right there in our green apple-colored office. I felt that familiar whisper of hope and strength, the calming warmth that comes with His presence. Terri's prayer refocused my heart on Him and stuck with me throughout the night and through the days following.

CHAPTER 6

Hello & Goodbye

The sun washed over us in yellows and oranges as we arrived at the hospital at 6:20 am on Friday, June 11th. My stepmom and dad had driven me, and my mom would meet us inside. For as long as I could remember Cyndi was the documentarian of our family, especially now that we had a video recorder. From birthdays to dance recitals, she found it easy to make commentary and remembered to take videos and pictures of memories we knew we would want one day. I'm so grateful for that gift.

She began our Kaylee documentary right there in the parking lot. Still standing by our white van, with my stuffed Eeyore from Disney World in hand revealing still how much of a child I was myself, she asked me questions. I was quiet, as usual, barely audible as I answered that today was going to be Kaylee's birthday. I didn't exactly like to be filmed, and I still don't, but I'm glad she captured memories throughout our childhood and especially during Kaylee's hospital stay. She quietly filmed me checking in, settling into birthing room number 231, and throughout the day when milestones happened. She and my mom also took turns writing down details of when things happened and taking lots of pictures. I was so grateful for their teamwork and support, coming together for me. Two moms, two different roles, two different personalities. I loved them equally, and I had an inkling that perhaps this is what open adoption might be like for Kaylee if all went as we planned. I already admired Christine so much, and I hoped we could be this teamwork support in Kaylee's life one day.

Dr. Hayes came in to go over the plan for the day. She was a younger doctor with blond hair, and I felt comfortable with her. I was grateful the doctor on staff that day was a female. Though the male doctors I'd seen during my prenatal visits were great, I was relieved that my most intimate moments of birth would be with a female. She knew my situation, and the kindness shone through eyes framed by her thick dark-rimmed glasses.

At 8:15 am, Pitocin was administered to begin my induction. As I felt the coolness of the IV fluids flowing into my veins, I began to feel nervous. What would contractions feel like? Would I be able to handle them? I hadn't taken any labor preparation classes since I was set on having an epidural to numb the pain as soon as possible. I also didn't want to be the only teen in a hospital couples' class—awkward. At the time, I had no idea pregnancy centers existed that taught classes for people like me. But had I known, I still don't think I would have taken a class, even then. I was set on an epidural as my only coping skill. The only other thing I brought to help me was motivational pictures to tape beside my bed. I brought a picture from the summer before at Camp

Hanes where I had hiked a week on the Appalachian trail, a time when I felt a sense of accomplishment and pride, of overcoming. If I could do that, I could give birth.

At 9:15 am, they broke my water to get the contractions going quicker. It was a disgusting feeling, but I went along with anything they suggested to bring my baby into the world. At 10:10 am, I still felt comfortable, so I allowed Christine and Phil to visit while I rested in bed. We all talked for a while, but by the time they left at 11:40 am, I was beginning to hurt. I remembered my very first period when I was nearly twelve years old, just before starting seventh grade. I was in the backseat while we were in the McDonald's drive through when a cramp ripped through my abdomen, doubling me over as I cried in pain. Cyndi looked back at me and said, "That pain right there, remember it. That's what labor feels like." She was right.

The nurses gave me a shot of something in my IV to help dull the pain, which alleviated somewhat but made me extremely loopy and tired. That helped me to rest until I could get my epidural, but I did not like how it made me feel. Rays of sunshine poured through the window, broken up through the blinds, and the lights were dim. The room was calm as I drifted in and out of sleep. We waited.

The day dragged on. I hadn't been able to eat since the night before, and I was starving. Watery broth with barely any flavor and ice chips could only satisfy for so long. We talked about what my first meal would be, and I asked for a Char-Grill burger with ketchup, mustard, and pickles on it and fries. That would be my reward, and I couldn't wait!

Finally, I got an epidural in place at 3:30 pm. I cried through contractions and tried to be still as they instructed. I believe they even told me, "If you can't be still, we can't do this." The nurses and my two moms comforted me as I tried my best not to squirm. I certainly did not enjoy the process of the epidural but the relief was worth it. I could see the contractions rising and falling on our monitor, but couldn't feel them. Sweet relief! At one point, Kaylee's heart rate dropped, and they worried for her. They attached an internal monitor to her head to make sure she would remain stable. If she didn't, we would have to do a c-section. Things progressed, Kaylee was well, and by 7:45 pm, it was time to start pushing.

I pushed and pushed, unsure how exactly to do that when I couldn't even feel my legs. They brought a giant mirror out to help me have a focal point, and I watched Kaylee enter the world slowly. My mom on my left side, Cyndi on my right, I pushed until she was finally born at 9 pm on the dot. They brought her to my chest, still covered in birthing goo, and she was the most beautiful thing I had ever seen. *My baby. I made this!* I felt elated that she was finally here and that I had made it through birth just fine. I couldn't speak yet, but I hoped that the love bursting from within me would reach her soul. She was so, so loved.

Cyndi, of course, filmed and photographed what she could. She somehow simultaneously encouraged me through labor all while holding a camera in her left hand and the video camera in her right. "You did it, Leah!" she cheered, voice crackling as she held back tears.

Kaylee and I were cleaned off, and my seven-pound two-ounce baby came back to my arms bundled up in the classic white, blue, and pink hospital blanket and hat. My dad joined us to meet her for the first time, and we took the next hour to be just us, her birth family surrounding her with love and in awe of this new little person. We each held her and took pictures with her.

I still couldn't speak much (which isn't shocking for me as a quiet person). Instead, I studied her every feature. Her blonde wispy hair and deep blue eye color. Her lips that clearly were not mine, and her nose that was. The perfect mixture she seemed to be of my family and her birth father's. She had a tiny freckle on her pinky that disappeared later, and we all marveled at the tiny spot. How can a baby already have a freckle? I stroked her velvety cheek thinking in my head over and over *I love you, I love you, I love you.* I prayed and thanked the Lord, feeling the joy and strength from every prayer that had been prayed for me that day throughout the country. Finally, I looked up at my parents and whispered, "She was meant to be theirs."

As much as I loved her, as much as I wished I could be her mom, I still knew in the depth of my soul they were meant to be her parents. The peace guiding me by the Holy Spirit was still there. I think we all wondered how it would be once I saw and held her in person—would it change my mind? For some birth mothers, it does, and they have every right. But for me, I only felt assurance yet again that this was the right thing for us. That peace continued to be the strength keeping me afloat through the approaching wave of grief.

It was nearly midnight before I was settled into a new room on the mother and baby hall and feeling better after delivery. Someone retrieved the Chargrill burger I desperately wanted, and I had recovered some energy. I felt ready for Christine and Phil to meet her then. I had wanted them to meet as soon as possible to begin bonding, but I was glad I took my time with her first. As Gray reminded me: they would have forever with her; these hospital days were my time.

Propped up in my hospital bed, I watched as Kaylee was placed into Christine's arms for the first time. The awe and wonder upon her face as she gazed down at Kaylee brought me joy. Yet, what struck me most was when Phil had his turn to hold her. From across the room, I watched the way he cradled her in his arms as he stood and swayed, gently and quietly introducing himself. A single tear streamed down his cheek as he fell in love with his new baby girl. That, right there, is what I wanted for her. A dad who loved her and would always be there for her. "She's already got me wrapped around her little finger," he sighed with a soft smile. Having a present father was a huge reason that I made my adoption decision. Observing him with her, entrusting him to be her protector and guide in life, I felt that familiar peace and assurance yet again. She was meant to be theirs. This was her family.

My mom stayed in the uncomfortable hospital lounging chair that night, both of us exhausted from the day. Of course, it wasn't solid sleep with nurses coming in and out to check on me and press intolerably against my uterus to make sure it was healing well.

OUR FIRST SATURDAY

The next day, Saturday the 12th, was a visiting day for many people. I asked several people to come to visit so they would have a chance to meet her before Kaylee left with Christine and Phil. Aunts, neighbors who were like family, my siblings, Grandparents, and even my favorite teacher, Mrs. Dunn, showed up to love on us. I loved showing off this beautiful little girl, my precious creation. She was more alert, and we could see her deep blue eyes curiously taking in the new world around her. We spent the day taking as many pictures and videos as possible. These photos would become a source of comfort to reflect on over and over through my grieving and help me to remember details now as the memories blur with time.

The best visitor of all drove thirteen hours to be by my side, my Breanna from Indiana, my Bre, as I call her. She had become such a close friend since meeting in our online group, and her adoption was a model of what I hoped ours would look like. We were similar in many ways from loving pot roast as our favorite homemade meal to the birth father of our children having the same name. Breanna and her mom drove hours to be a support to me and my family, being the only two people in the room to truly understand the emotional impact we were facing as a family. It meant the world to me that they both would sacrifice time, money, and emotional energy to be present for me, their gift of support priceless.

Getting to meet Bre in person was like meeting a long-lost friend; our souls knew each other deeply already, and we picked up right away as if we had known each other for years and not for mere minutes. Having her near was like a safety net, knowing she could advise me and listen to me in ways no one else could. There is nothing like being in the room with another birth mother who knows the profound joys and aches of adoption though the situations surrounding vary. Aside from the gift of her presence, she brought Kaylee's family and I gifts to honor the occasion. One was a matching fleece teddy bear blanket for both of us that she had hand-tied, which became well-used by both our families over the years. That blanket brought me years of warmth and comfort, both as a reminder of her friendship and in knowing that a few hours away, my little girl might be wrapped up in hers, too.

Of course, I was still physically exhausted from giving birth so my parents made sure to protect my time. Emotionally I was still riding the oxytocin high and was soaking in every moment with Kaylee. I kept Kaylee with me for most of my time in the hospital. Kaylee and I took naps together, my stepmom watching over us. I fed her bottles and changed her clothes when she spit up all over them. Her parents came to visit as well, and we shared time together, they fed her and changed her diapers too. We joked that since I was so short, and Christine was very tall that I was little mama and she was big mama. The atmosphere to me felt like a family reunion, a good one! I genuinely enjoyed everyone surrounding me and wanted them there. The smiles captured in the pictures were authentic.

I felt secure and supported throughout my stay, I'm sure the advocacy from my family and social worker was a huge part of that. The staff seemed equipped to handle our unique situation. Everyone was kind and professional, not judgmental or pushy in any way. One nurse felt like a loving Grandma figure to me. Wanda was probably in her later fifties, with curled short brown hair as many Grandmas have, and thin oval glasses perched on her nose. Her joyous way of caring for us felt like she saw me as a mother, too, and was an encouragement. I knew she had seen a lot in her time as a nurse, and she shared her wisdom with us. She prompted us to take pictures of her tiny wrinkled feet to remember just how tiny they were. She posed my hands in a heart around them as she had seen other moms do. She's the only nurse that we have a photo of, so I'm guessing Cyndi wanted to remember her kindness as well.

For the most part, the staff talked to me as the mom. After all, I had not signed any relinquishment papers yet. I was their priority to look after and Kaylee was my child. Yet, there was one nurse who didn't address me much in regard to Kaylee's care. She spoke to Christine and Phil with directions, not me. That irked us a tad since I was in the room, too, and caring for her while at the hospital, but in the grand scheme of things, it was a small moment. Other birth mothers have had far worse treatment and judgment, and I felt grateful for my positive experience and the people around me.

Breanna and I had our first sleepover that Saturday night. I watched her from my bed snuggling my little girl in her arms on the stiff hospital chair that was serving as her bed for the evening. Grateful for both of our daughters that brought us together to that moment, I ended the night with a full heart.

SUNDAY, NOT FUN DAY

While Saturday was filled with the highs after birth, friendship, and family, Sunday was when the reality of loss came collapsing into the beauty of new life. Saturday felt like I could hold up my hand to grief and keep it at a distance to enjoy the moments in front of me. I didn't think about the tomorrow when goodbye would come. I felt the comfort of time between birth and relinquishment on Saturday. But Sunday, I could no longer hold back the flood of emotions. I still felt a deep peace about my choice in adoption, but now it was time to put it into writing. I didn't feel pressured by my family, my social worker, or Kaylee's parents. In fact, they made sure that I didn't feel their pressure.

Christine and Phil asked to speak to me alone Sunday morning. Pulling up chairs beside my bed as my family exited the room, I felt unsure what this was about. I hesitantly sat up straighter in my hospital bed and fluffed my covers to ease my awkwardness.

Phil looked at me with the kindness of a father in his eyes and began speaking in his usual comforting yet assertive way, "Leah, we wanted time with you alone before anything is signed to make sure this is right for *you*. This is your baby, your decision. You don't owe us anything. We want to make sure that you feel at peace with adoption and with us. We are here for you, either way. Yes, we would be sad if you decide to parent her, but we will be okay. She is your baby first."

I don't remember what I responded with exactly, but I know that their humility in open-handedly loving me and our baby girl so well left me feeling in awe of them. This couple that was unable to have children biologically was *so close* to adding to their family... and they were willing to walk away if it isn't the right situation for everyone involved? This conversation only sealed my heart to theirs more completely, a seal of trust and respect, of love and honor. It assured me of their integrity and character yet again. It secured my decision and peace even more, and that's what I told them.

After they left, it was time to sign the paperwork to make this plan official. Gray pulled up the hospital tray so I would have a flat surface to look at the papers and sign. Breanna stood to the left of my bed, tissues in hand, personally understanding the grip of grief I was feeling. I don't know who else was in the room, but Bre's presence was a comfort to my soul. Gray informed me of my rights and what I was choosing to legally put into place. My heart shattered into a million pieces and revolted as I read the words before me, yet still contained within the boundaries of peace that I clung to. *"I hereby relinquish all rights to said child and surrender said child..."* Oh, how my heart ached. I loved her and didn't want to do this, but I still knew it was the right thing. *"I understand that when the adoption is final, all of my rights and duties with respect to the minor will be extinguished, and all other aspects of my legal relationship with the minor child will be terminated."*

Making the decision of adoption is one thing. Choosing a family for your child to be raised by is one thing. Seeing the words in black and white and signing your name is another altogether. It's a devastating reality. No longer is it just talk, but action. The wording can make you feel unfit and unloving as a mother, yet I still knew despite the legal phrases on that document, I loved Kaylee and was choosing a life for her to break cycles. To give her more.

Tears streamed, and my hand shook as the pen hovered over the signature lines. Hesitating, I prayed Kaylee would one day understand why I made this decision. I prayed to the Lord that He would do as I felt He had promised me. That He would turn this grief and use it for glory. That her parents would fulfill their promises and that while this legally may be the end of my mothering, I still could be present in her life. I signed that paper, trusting them and the Lord to be faithful. I surrendered yet again my will for God's will.

AN ADOPTION CEREMONY

After taking time to collect myself emotionally and rest, we prepared for the ceremony I had planned months ago. I envisioned a time to dedicate Kaylee to the Lord and bless our new adoption relationship. Much like a wedding ceremony is only the beginning of a marriage, this would mark the beginning of our lifelong commitment to one another. Gray warned me that this might be too much emotionally, but I insisted. I wanted to celebrate a new beginning, even if my heart was breaking.

A cake was bought. The room was encircled by family and friends. Christine and Phil sat on chairs to the left of my bed sharing the spotlight with me. Kaylee lay asleep in my lap upon a white blanket one of my Grandmothers had crocheted for her. I sensed each person's love and support, their awe and ache within the same breath of what they were witnessing. Many brought baby clothes and other gifts for Kaylee's family and mementos for me. I used this time to also present the gift I made for Christine and Kaylee–a matching heart charm that represented our open adoption. Christine's charm and mine each had our initials on front, with Kaylee's new initials on the back. Kaylee's charm had her initials on the front with the back displaying both of ours, honoring us as both of her moms. From the front, it looked like a normal engraved heart charm, but I loved knowing that hidden from view and close to my heart was Kaylee's name, a secret just for me, unless I wanted to share it. I wore it every day for years.

I invited my youth pastor to say a few words. She opened her well-worn black bible to 1 Corinthians 13 and began reading,

> Love is patient, love is kind. It does not envy, it does not boast, it is not proud. It does not dishonor others, it is not self-seeking, it is not easily angered, it keeps no record of wrongs. Love does not delight in evil but rejoices with the truth. It always protects, always trusts, always hopes, always perseveres. Love never fails. (1 Corinthians 13:4–8a, NIV)

She remarked how this passage is typically used in weddings but how beautiful of a reminder these words are for any relationship—especially an adoption relationship. A sacrificial love for one another, always seeking to do that is honoring for one another. A love that trusts and hopes and perseveres on behalf of the little person we all love at the center.

Then my Grandpa, God bless him, spoke up and offered a prayer over us. It was sentimental and kind but also emotional. Again, I realized my choices had inflicted grief on others beyond me. I couldn't hold in my tears any longer. His words cracked through the façade of joy I wanted to uphold, and I began to cry. My little brother came up to me and asked, "Why are you crying, Leah?" I'm sure he felt confused in his innocence by the complexity of this situation. Were we supposed to be happy or sad? What was going on?

I replied simply in a whisper through my tears, "Because I don't get to be her mom." He rubbed Kaylee's soft hair and patted my arm telling me it would be okay.

After that, Gray was proven right, and I needed space to breathe. The crowd I had wanted there now felt suffocating; the grief was swallowing me. My parents shooed everyone to the hallway, and the closest of people remained by my side: my mom, my stepmom, my Bre, and my social worker.

Looking back, I don't regret the ceremony. It served the purpose I intended and created the memories I had hoped it would. If I did it all over again, I think I would keep it smaller and more intimate. Too many people in a room, no matter how much I loved them and wanted them there, with big emotions was too much.

The evening ended better with my support system in place and the good news of more time together. I was released from the hospital's care Sunday afternoon, but Kaylee's doctor was concerned about hip dysplasia—a clicking in her hip socket. Kaylee would move to the pediatric unit, and I would be allowed to spend another night with her! While we were concerned about her hip, I praised the Lord for the gift of more time with her.

Christine and I made a plan to spend the night together and care for her in the new hospital room. I had the bed since I was still recovering, and she slept in a recliner. She brought us sleepover necessities like snacks and nail polish (though we didn't get to that part). I have no idea what we chatted about all night, but the comradery felt natural. We shared holding Kaylee, feeding her, changing her. We laughed. We told stories. We bonded. It was the perfect way to end our hospital time.

GOODBYE FOR NOW

The next morning Kaylee's hip was magically perfect, and she was released. I thanked the Lord for His mercies of extra time and healing. We all prepared to take pictures before leaving the hospital in the gardens downstairs. I put on a comfortable maternity dress that I had worn on Easter and put my hair up in a ponytail. Kaylee was dressed in the same pink outfit I had picked out months ago. I packed tangible memories away in my bag: her hospital bracelet, a blanket, a hat, a bottle, and a pacifier. Items of hers I would never use in my own home, but they would remind me of this time we had together.

Someone wheeled me downstairs in a chair per hospital policy, and we gathered for our photo shoot. Phil took a photo of me arriving and told me later during a visit, "I just couldn't understand how you could be smiling like that. It was just so beautiful and a testament to the Lord's joy." And it's true. While Sunday had been full of tears and grief, Monday I had woken up to His joy being my strength. The strength to say goodbye for now. The joy of our time together.

We took as many poses and pictures as possible with their family and mine. My favorite though has always been the one of Christine and I each kissing one of Kaylee's cheeks. She's asleep, mouth wide open, unaware of all that's happening around her, but I love how it displays our open adoption.

Finally, it was time to say goodbye. I chose to have them leave first. I tucked her into her checkered yellow and navy car seat, kissed her head and whispered how much I loved her. She still slept peacefully, unaware of all the decisions going on around her that would affect her life. Christine hugged me and choked back tears, "You know this is just goodbye for now. We will see you soon! I promise." That comforted me, again soothing my soul that they meant what they said, that I would see her again soon. Forever was too much to bear without her, but I could do "soon."

They handed me a gift bag as they left, which I opened in the car on the way home. They gifted me a yellow daisy journal, some pampering items, a card, and a little dachshund charm. It was simple, thoughtful, and perfect.

As Cyndi drove me home in our van, I was sad it was all over. I wasn't sure how I would cope in this new chapter. Yet, I felt deeply that I wasn't walking through my grief alone. I had, and still have, Jesus to hold my hand along the way. The weight of grief isn't so heavy when there is Someone with me to shoulder it, just as I had read in Matthew 11:28–30.

> *"Come to me, all you who are weary and burdened, and I will give you rest. Take my yoke upon you and learn from me; for I am gentle and humble in heart, and you will find rest for your souls. For my yoke is easy and my burden is light." (NIV)*

Part 3

THIS NEW LIFE

*"Therefore, if anyone is in Christ,
the new creation has come: The
old has gone, the new is here!"*

2 Corinthians 5:17, NIV

CHAPTER 7

The First Year

Arriving home empty-bellied and empty-handed was a heartbreaking new beginning. If you've ever experienced a miscarriage or stillbirth loss, it is a similar feeling. Having both lost a child through adoption and through a miscarriage a few years later, I can attest that they feel oddly similar. It's a sense of emptiness when there should be fullness and life. It was a triggering reminder that adoption is in fact loss— unnatural— even if it's what you feel is best in the circumstances, even with the peace of the Lord. In both losses, I felt peace, but that didn't mean I skipped past grieving what could have been.

There are physical reminders that your baby did exist and lived within you, like leaking milk, bleeding, a still swollen belly, and cramping, all which point to a birth with nothing to show for it. The dreams you had for your future together now look different than you'd planned.

Years later when I became a parenting mother, I remember how odd it felt to even be in a separate room from my newborn, let alone hours away. During postpartum recovery after Kaylee's birth, I felt that distance intensely. I felt literally empty. My stomach where she once nestled closely was still the size of my five-month belly, yet now it was lifeless and jiggly.

During pregnancy, she was a presence always with me in my day-to-day, now gone as if a death had occurred. Yet, she wasn't dead. She was alive and well in the home of the family I chose. What a complex reality.

I was lucky to be surrounded by a support system that honored my grief. Other birth mothers I've known have been forced to quickly "move on" and "forget this all happened." For years, that's how American birth mothers were treated, ushered into silence to pretend everything was fine. They were encouraged to never speak about it again, or perhaps only to speak when discovering safe places like birth mother groups. This "disenfranchised grief," as Dr. Doka termed this specific type of grief, has haunted every birth mother in some capacity.[7]

My family never shied away from talking about Kaylee or our feelings and supported me however they could. I believe that support is a huge reason I worked through my grieving easier and in healthier ways. I wasn't walking it alone. I wasn't silenced. Kaylee was a missing piece in all of our hearts, and that was honored. We celebrated the good parts together and cried together when it was difficult.

---

7 Doka, K. J. "Disenfranchised Grief in Historical and Cultural Perspective." In Handbook of Bereavement Research and Practice: Advances in Theory and Intervention, M. S. Stroebe, R. O. Hansson, H. Schut, & W. Stroebe (Eds.), (pp. 223–240). American Psychological Association, 2008. https://doi.org/10.1037/14498-011

Coming home from the hospital, my mother stayed nearby for a few days and made me my favorite comfort food. My family bought me summer cherries to eat and set me up in the prized living room recliner to rest, watch TV, and be with the family. That's where I spent many of my days following birth, snuggling with my puppies. They were weights to my empty arms and soothing for my soul.

While they set me up like a pampered queen for a while, I still, of course, battled tears and needed their comfort. I was sad that our hospital time was over. I grieved that this crescendo of excitement had passed and that now it was time to move on with life to find a new normal.

I loved having everyone surrounding me there like one big family, both at the hospital and after. I had felt whole, no one missing. Now that precious time was over and we all went our separate ways. My mom to one destination, me to another, and Kaylee to yet another. My heart was stretched apart to different parts of North Carolina, and it hurt.

My stepmom quickly printed photos of the hospital, and I relived the memories over and over as I flipped through them, choosing which ones I wanted to show off to my friends or display in my room. I had been gifted many flipbooks, albums, and frames to fill up, and I used them all proudly. The high of "I made her!" with the low of "I miss her so much" was a constant roller coaster, but having photos helped me remember again my decision and how loved I felt in those days.

One afternoon, a large package showed up on our doorstep. Cyndi brought it to me in the living room, "This has your name on it." I was baffled, who sent *me* something? The label read "Birth Mom Buds," but I had never heard of them and didn't order anything. I hesitantly opened the box to find gifts like a picture frame, a candle, lotion, and a CD with thoughtfully curated songs that reminded them of adoption. As lovely as it was to receive a gift... how did they know I had placed my child? When I posted in my adoption group, I found out the answer: another birth mom had given my name and address to the non-profit. I was so grateful! Birth Mom Buds quickly became another healing resource for me through annual retreats, friendships, and eventually my first public speaking role. The connections made there are ones that will forever be etched on my heart. There is nothing like being in a room with other birth mothers.

OUR FIRST VISIT

Still on pain pills from birth, at night I would have intense dreams. My chest was aching as my body begged for my baby to relieve the pressure and feed, yet she wasn't there. One night, I fell asleep on my back with a bag of ice on my chest to help soothe the pain and make the milk dry up. When it started to slip from my relaxed arms I had a dream that I was dropping my baby and she was gone. I woke up in a panic and terrified— *Where's my baby?!* Either

Cyndi heard me crying, or I asked her to come to help me. Either way, she came to sleep in my bed to be a comfort. Her closeness was needed. I didn't want to be alone. I wasn't used to being alone. I woke up crying many nights and for two weeks Cyndi was by my side, holding my hand under our pillows so I knew I wasn't alone.

Talking with Christine and Phil, knowing Kaylee was doing well, did help though. But the following week after her birth, I missed her so much that I requested a visit. They had told me from the beginning, "Just ask. If we can arrange it, we will." So I took them up on that offer and took a giant uncomfortable leap by asking for what my heart needed.

Now, keep in mind that in North Carolina, I had ten days to revoke my rights and undo the adoption plan. Though knowing I could revoke our agreement was a comfort if I felt I had made a mistake, I just wanted to see her again, hold her, and know she was okay. I never felt like I would revoke, but I know the fearful thought crossed their minds as they waited in the limbo of legal finality. Yet, they said yes anyway. At the risk of me changing my mind when I saw Kaylee again, Christine and Phil trusted the Lord with Kaylee, too. They opened their hearts and door yet again, staying true to the character they had been showing to me through the months.

My dad and I loaded up my 1992 Honda Civic for our three hour road trip. It hurt my recovering bottom to sit there that long, but I didn't care. I was on the way to see Kaylee! Finally arriving at their one-story home, I felt my heart become whole again. Even now that she is grown, being near Kaylee still brings me a sense of completeness.

Her family welcomed us in and gave us a tour. I quickly saw the nursery we had designed together over the phone and through photos. They had taken the bedding I picked out with pink and green butterflies and yellow flowers to coordinate the whole room. The walls were painted bubblegum pink with butterflies hand painted as a border. Walking into her room I saw on the left side was her wooden crib with the bedding I loved, and on the right side was a twin daybed covered in a coordinating green gingham handmade cover.

"This is where you can sleep when you come to visit in the future," they told me.

The magnitude of their generosity in including me in their lives was hard to fully comprehend. It wasn't "normal," and it certainly wasn't typical in adoption relationships, especially in 2004 when open adoption was barely known. It wasn't taught to them in an educational class at our agency. It wasn't in a book or on a blog post. They acted instinctively with Jesus's love flowing from their hearts. They invited me into their hearts and lives, and it showed through their actions.

During that visit, we were all exhausted from our mix of traveling and their newborn nights. At one point, every single one of us fell asleep in their living room! From Kaylee and her brother, to all three adults, we somehow all managed to take a nap. Talk about reaching a new level of comfort with one another!

Feeling the weight of my baby once again in my arms and getting to feed her a bottle again helped to soothe my heart. Seeing her new environment with her attentive parents also helped me. This visit wasn't one that made me change my mind; it assured me yet again. Turning to wave goodbye when it was time to leave, I remember looking at her house and family waving goodbye back thinking, *She is where she is meant to be*. I felt at peace.

WRITING BLOSSOMS

I kept a journal growing up, often in simple spiral-bound notebooks. However, during my pregnancy and with the growing internet community, I started sharing private blog journal entries with a select few close friends, like my Bre. Those entries became a preferred way to cope and process my feelings while also documenting what was going on in my teenage world.

When I wanted to keep my feelings private, I wrote in the hardback journal that Gray had given me at the hospital. It had a beautiful poem inside that spoke so well of grief and how, after a while, it changes and shifts. I had never had a "real" journal before, and it seemed natural to pour my changing life, sorrows, triumphs, and prayers into it.

However, within the pages of the yellow daisy journal that Christine and Phil had given me, I began writing to Kaylee when I missed her, and the evidence of grief was especially present:

June 27th, 2004

"Why can't you be here with me?" I keep asking myself. I know the answer to my question, but the pain is still there. I miss you so much. I hate I've had only a few hours with you, and her parents have had weeks. My arms feel empty, yet you are there for them to hold whenever they feel the need to hold you. I have nothing, only memories and pictures.

I hate feeling like you are not "mine" now. Yes, I have a daughter, but she's far away. She is perfectly content without me. She doesn't even know I'm her mother... at least that's what it feels like. People tell me you know my voice and scent. But do you now? Now that I haven't seen you in over a week?

July 3rd, 2004

I saw you today for my second visit. You are three weeks old and one day! Time goes by so fast, yet it seems like it has been longer.

Oh, it was so good to hold you again. I fed you a bottle and burped you. For a moment, it felt as if you were "mine." For a moment, my arms didn't feel empty, and a piece of my heart returned.

You and I had time all to ourselves while others played in the park. It was so nice. You were half dreaming, half awake. You would smile and peek open your eyes for a moment. You are so beautiful! I talked to you and told you how pretty your smiles were. How wonderful it was for it to be just me and you again... just for a moment.

When we said our goodbyes again, I still knew you are where you belong. I love you, and I'm sending you kisses!

For a moment, it felt as though you were mine again

My arms did not feel empty and a piece of my heart returned

Of course, that piece left again

when we went our separate ways but for a moment...

I was complete

September 2nd, 2004

My last visit with you was almost a month ago. It was at the beginning of August for four days. It was so wonderful!

But for right now I am missing you so bad. I miss holding you and looking into your beautiful eyes. You have grown so much. I didn't realize until I looked at your pictures from the hospital how much you have changed. You will be three months old on my 17th birthday. I am so glad you and your parents will be here. I miss them a lot too! I love talking with your mom and hearing your dad's stories. Blake is pretty funny, too. :)

I just got off the phone with Breanna. She always helps me feel better when I'm feeling sad. I usually call your mom, too. She is always a big reassurance for me. I can't wait to see you and your family again!

Writing became a lifeline for me, along with my growing relationship with the Lord. It felt as if writing became a gift from Him, and the words began to bubble from within, pouring onto various pages. I eventually began to write more publicly with a blog as well, hoping to reach more people with this unique experience I was working my way through. Within the gaps of healing came words that gave me purpose, a new mission. I knew I needed to share my journey even if I didn't know what my message was quite yet. Even at sixteen, I felt the whisper of the Lord to my heart, *"This will be a book one day."* It was a dream-seed planted long ago that is blooming here today. I knew our story had a purpose beyond just our little adoption triad; it would ripple through society and shift hearts. Over time, God kept providing opportunities to share, but it all started with writing for myself to let out my grief, just as Gray had encouraged me to do while I was pregnant. Writing was my pressure release.

A NEW WAY TO LIVE

Kaylee became my motivation to change and do better. I wanted to make her proud of me. Choosing adoption was a means of a second chance for Kaylee and myself, and I wanted to prove it was worthy of the sacrifice I had made. I was determined to be this new version of me that I was becoming, and I pressed into learning about God's character and His grace and obeying the nudges of the Holy Spirit to change my life. I made every effort to "put on the new self" as I had read in my Bible.

> *"That, however, is not the way of life you learned when you heard about Christ and were taught in him in accordance with the truth that is in Jesus. You were taught, with regard to your former way of life, to put off your old self, which is being corrupted by its deceitful desires; to be made new in the attitude of your minds; and to put on the new self, created to be like God in true righteousness and holiness."*
> *Ephesians 4:20–24, NIV*

The genres of music I used to blast in my room before now rubbed me the wrong way, so I tucked them away in an old binder and went to CD stores to find new music. While my music had shifted previously a little, this time I felt convicted to put everything away that wasn't clean and God-honoring. I wanted to surround myself with reminders of God's truths and be lifted up, especially as my soul was healing.

In church, music changed for me as well. My whole life, Cyndi would nudge me gently with her elbow and mouth "sing" at me. But, I didn't feel the words, want to sing, or understand why I needed to. They were just words on a screen that hung empty. Yet, now those words went straight to my heart, and I willingly sang in gratitude and worship of His love for me. I had experienced Him, and I couldn't help but sing now. Driving back and forth the hours it took to get to my mom's or to visit Kaylee became hours of worship and time with the Lord.

In the spring of 2005, I was baptized by the same pastor who had shepherded my family through the hardships of the previous year. As the crowd surrounding the pool sang "Amazing Grace," the pool transformed from recreational to holy. True to the nature of baptism, it was an outward expression and declaration of my love for Jesus and a new way of living. Many people there that day knew my journey to that point, and I felt surrounded by their love yet again. As my face emerged from the water, I felt the Lord's peace settle over my soul. Ironically, I wore a bathing suit with a Bible verse t-shirt that Samuel's mom had gifted to me in the previous months. We had some contact outside of Samuel, and I knew she was proud of me, too.

I read my Bible often with a new zeal in how it felt alive, speaking right to me. I joined youth groups and read Christian books, soaking up how to live in this new way. I wanted to know how to live differently, especially how to do romantic relationships differently. I was certainly in no hurry to get into a new relationship any time soon. Steering clear of drama and heartache was one of my main goals in life in this season.

For the first time since childhood, the desire to constantly need a boyfriend wasn't there. For the first time, I understood how Jesus can truly satisfy your soul. I felt drawn to the Lord in this season of singleness as I pressed into His character and allowed Him to shape me like clay. Sure, I found boys cute still, but I also had much higher standards and no one seemed worthy of dating now. It also felt like the Lord protected me as no one was really interested in me either. It was completely different from my old school where I often had my pick each month. But here, perhaps no one wanted to be with the girl who was pregnant, much like Hester Prynne in *The Scarlet Letter*, but I liked it that way. The temptation was rarely there, so it was easier to stay on the straight and narrow path. When I was in the rare tempting situation, usually when returning to my mom's for a visit and seeing old friends, I was always able to stop. That identity wasn't me anymore, and I wasn't willing to risk the heartache or shame again.

Now, this was the prime time of Purity Culture, which has since been known to cause some damage to Christians' mentality on sex, and I certainly have misconceptions to untangle from it. Yet, in my personal journey at seventeen years old, Eric and Leslie Ludy's books were a revolutionary mindset for me. When I felt ready to date again, I wanted to make sure I approached it differently. I desired to be the "lily among the valley" in Song of Solomon 2:1, a beautiful soul blooming in wait. Their books spoke of "taking trash" out of your heart so you wouldn't be held back emotionally when you did meet the one God has for you. They also assured that we are never too far beyond God's grace. I needed those messages to help ease the shame I felt about my choices previously. Their books didn't make me feel unworthy or bad because of my past. Rather, their books gave me a new sense of direction and reassurance that I was inherently worthy because of Jesus' love. Because I was trusting the Lord in this new chapter of life, it gave me hope that I could still have a love story like the Ludys'.

Their love story also gave me hope that there were still good, Jesus-following young men out there who would want the same life as me. I prepared myself while waiting for him, wanting to be a better and healthier version of myself when he was brought into my life. I wrote to my future husband in my journal and dreamed of what he might be like one day. When I felt lonely, I pressed into the Lord even more, trusting Him with my future. I was determined to let God write my love story, just like the Ludy's. I had surrendered my life, and my child, to Jesus' plan and I could see how He was working all that for good. I figured He could do the same with my love life.

ONE WHOLE YEAR

Kaylee's first birthday came just as quickly as her pregnancy had flown by. Having just finished my senior year of high school and graduated with good grades, I felt joyful and thriving. My new life had focused on healing, my schoolwork, my friendships, my new job at Limited Too, and my relationship with Kaylee's parents. It was working well for me. I felt like I was proving to myself and others that I was a new person and making the most of my second chance.

Reflecting on her first birthday, my heart nearly burst at how blessed I felt. I felt I didn't deserve this amount of trust and inclusion, and I often still feel guilty that I have this incredible relationship while other birth mothers are left sitting in silence, their questions unanswered. Yet, our first year went far better than I ever imagined, with promises not only kept but exceeded by her family.

Once I felt comfortable driving longer distances with my new driver's license, I began to spend weekends with Kaylee and her family nearly once a month and on longer school holidays. Those memories were the building blocks of our relationship, adding to those we had laid during pregnancy and our hospital experience. In those everyday moments together, we built a deeper friendship.

Christine and Phil were always so thoughtful and intentional, treating me like an extension of their family. During one visit, Christine saved feeding Kaylee solids for the first time so that I could witness it as well. Of course, many milestones like crawling and walking can't be planned, but Christine included me whenever she could. They had professional photos taken of just me and Kaylee one time. Often they would call a random day with a new update or just to say "Her eyes looked just like yours today!" I felt treasured, honored, and respected in my unique role in their life.

My favorite memories were when we would sit around their table after dinner and just talk. Kaylee's parents, especially her dad, always had a fun story to share that revealed Kaylee's blossoming personality or a new milestone met. Phil would impart his wisdom often, becoming like a father figure to me as well. He'd talk about wise finances or share inspirational stories from lessons learned in their past.

It was also in those moments that Phil encouraged me to stay on a good path in life. "You know, we want Kaylee to be able to call you when she's a teen and mad at us so she can run to you as a safe place. But, we want to make sure you stay on a healthy path so that she's got a stable place to turn to." That motivated me to keep going as I was, healing and staying focused on the Lord, proving I was a different person and worthy of this relationship.

We talked about our vision for the future and how our relationship would grow. Even when Kaylee was an infant, we were dreaming of what life would look like in open adoption. It was all unknown; we didn't have examples to look to years ahead, just dreams and a foundation laid piece by piece over time.

Coming from a split home, I didn't have many examples of solid marriage and family relationships. Of course, my dad and Cyndi were one example that I could observe up close, but another important one was Christine and Phil. They became a model for me of how I hoped I could be in a healthy marriage one day with Christ at the center. I aspired to grow up to be like them in how they loved the Lord and others well (like how they love me). Watching how they cared for their children and each other was a beautiful example. I would attend church with them over the years and be introduced as Kaylee's birth mom to their friends. "Oh, we've heard so much about you!" It always feels good to know that they talk about me and that my role is known to others. It was never a secret in my home, nor in theirs.

While my relationship with her parents was growing and I found so much joy in their mentorship and friendship, seeing Kaylee so often was a huge piece of my healing as well. Whenever the pang of missing her touched my heart, I could reach out to hear an update or see a picture. Or, I would thumb through the pictures her parents had printed for me every few months— they made doubles of everything for me! The visits every month or two always satisfied the ache. It didn't take away my grief, my heart still was wounded and mending, but having visits and communication was like a balm to my soul. It soothed me so that I could keep going.

Still being a part of Kaylee's life to where she knew my face and fell asleep on me and getting to experience everyday moments with her was so helpful. Her mom was her mom, but when I was around, I always tried to be helpful and give them a break in ways that I could. Christine and I would share mothering together. I would get up with Kaylee and Blake early in the mornings to let Christine and Phil sleep in. I played with Kaylee and kept her entertained. It was as much for them as it was for me, and they allowed me space to treasure her. Those visits also reminded me yet again how I was very much not ready to be a mother and how exhausting it was emotionally and physically! It truly was the best of both worlds.

They even let me babysit several times. One time, Phil came home from work, sat down in his brown lazy boy and chuckled, "You wouldn't believe the comments I got at work today when I told them Kaylee's birth mom was babysitting her. '*What?! Aren't you afraid she's going to run off with her while you're gone?*' I told them, 'Well who better else to babysit her? She loves her as much as we do!'" And that was the truth. We all love her immensely and want the best for her. It also was encouraging to hear how much trust they had in me and how positively they share our relationship with others. They were educating people around them as much as I was.

The night of Kaylee's first birthday, I was able to stay the night in that twin little bed in her room once again. After a long day of traveling, partying, socializing, and reminiscing with our families— even my Bre joined us— I needed time to process. It's hard to explain how your heart can be so full of gratitude, yet also grieve at the same time. She had fallen asleep hours ago, but I scooped her up and held her anyway. I needed to be close. I needed to hold her and remember the events of the year before.

Then, I laid her back down in her crib and found a piece of paper from her parents' office desk to write this letter for her to read one day:

June 11th, 2005

I never dreamed I could be filled with so much love as I have for you. Not only are you the cutest little girl, but you are also blossoming into such an amazing girl with a wonderful personality. You are sounded by love; God surely smiles down on this mixed family! I feel like the luckiest person alive. Because of you and God's grace, a whole new light has been cast on my life. I've met amazing friends, traveled to new places, gained family members, and loved like I've never loved before I became a birth mom.

These past few days I have been blessed to spend a lot of time with you. Your parents are amazing like that and allow me to enjoy you as I know they do. That is why I am so lucky! Many birth moms don't experience the wonders of their birth children. I've been so blessed to experience feeding you, playing with you, and yes, even diaper changes. I have loved every minute and will continue to. I treasure our time together always. These past few days you've fallen asleep in my arms several times; those are my most precious memories with you— well, close to the huge smile you give me. As you slept, I rocked and thought about a year (and one hour) ago, the very first time I saw and held you. You were the most beautiful thing I've seen. Last night rocking you to sleep, all I could think was, "Oh, Lord! I love this girl!" I thank Him every day for bringing you and your parents into my life.

It boggles my mind that it has already been a year. It has flown by.

We've both learned and grown so much, and it's all been amazing. This is just the beginning of a beautiful journey, and I am so blessed to be a part of it! I love you always!

-Birth mommy Leah

CHAPTER 8

Falling Down Again

If my sixteenth year was my life turning point, and my seventeenth year was learning to heal and thrive again, then my eighteenth year started out feeling like a reward for my hard work and turned-around life.

After graduating high school, I spent the summer working and visiting Kaylee. In August, I packed up my room in large tupperware boxes packed into my little Honda and headed to the mountains. I applied to only one college, just *knowing* it was the one for me and praying I would get in. At the time, I wanted to pursue social work because I wanted to be to birth moms one day what Gray was in my life— helpful, healing, kind, and empowering. Appalachian State University had the courses I needed but, most importantly, the environment I craved. I wanted a small college, and my soul felt drawn to those Blue Ridge Mountains once more.

The funny thing is, when I was growing up, I hated Boone. My heart would revolt, and a lump would appear in my throat. I never wanted to go back due to the bad memories I had stashed away in my core memories. Yet somehow, the Lord softened my heart and told me, *Go to App State. Trust me.* So I went. And I was excited!

135

Aside from the fact that my mom and dad had attended here, so had Gray and Kaylee's mom. It felt like home to me and like carrying on a tradition of people I loved. Even better, I was assigned to live in the all-girls' dorm, White Hall. Remember, I didn't want boys around. I didn't want the temptation. I wanted to focus on my studies and the Lord. This happened to be the exact dormitory that Kaylee's mom lived in as well! I felt God-winks were all over this new chapter of my life, especially once I got my roommate assignment.

Facebook had just been invented in 2005, and I was among the first users, excited to finally have access to this then-exclusive college-restricted platform. Of course, when I got my roommate's name, I looked her up right away. Lindsay, I discovered, lived near me. We also realized that her mom and my aunt were best friends in high school. Finding this out, we planned our first meeting at our house before heading off to college together. It served as a reunion for the long-lost best friends as well!

And if that wasn't enough to assure me that this was the place for me, I also found *my* long-lost best friend from when I went to Kindergarten in Boone. Jessica had stayed in Boone all those years with her family and was now a freshman at App, too. I emailed her, and we instantly picked back up where we left off thirteen years before. She also had become a Christian, so she was a big help in getting plugged into a faith-based community in the area. Through Facebook, I had also found other acquaintances from past school years, too. I felt so grateful that the Lord was setting me up with a community and that this shy girl wouldn't be facing everything completely alone.

In August, Lindsay and I moved in. Our families shopped and decorated our dorm together and made it as cozy as it could be with what's allowed. Our dorm was freshly remodeled at the time and was one of the few with air conditioners! In the first months of college life, we stuck together and made friends. I spent time with other friends like Jessica occasionally, but often it was Lindsay and me who ate together in the dining hall. At least, it was that way until October came.

Fall break had just ended, and I was sitting at the covered AppleCart bus stop bench at the State Farm lot where all the freshmen have to park their cars waiting for the bus. Ironically, I was on the phone with Samuel at the time. I know I haven't mentioned him much, and there isn't really much to say after Kaylee came along. But, we had reached a cordial point, and for a while, I kept a distant relationship with him for Kaylee's sake. He didn't have or desire a relationship with her, but I felt like I needed to maintain some kind of connection in case she ever needed that one day. He wouldn't talk to her parents, but he would talk to me. And truthfully, there was still a ping of loss there and attraction. I logically didn't want to be with him since we were on very different life paths, and I was still hurt by him not being there for me, but when you create a child together, there's still a string of connection that's hard to cut loose.

This moment is ironic because just a few feet away, my future husband, Mark, was watching me thinking, *Wow, she's pretty. I want to get to know her*. With his hands in his classic black and yellow App State hoodie, pretending to be listening to his friend talking beside him, he felt a deep knowing that I was going to be someone special in his life.

I didn't notice him, though. I was busy with my phone call on my tiny flip phone, internally wondering why I was even talking to Samuel when I knew he wasn't the guy for me. It was a tug of war of knowing what I needed to do but couldn't do yet; I knew I needed to completely cut him out of my life. We had only seen each other one time since I'd moved in with my dad, and that visit reminded me why I had moved on. Despite all the changing I had done and despite my now higher standards, I still liked the attention from a safe distance.

The next day, my roommate and I were leaving the dining hall when I glanced through the window back into the cafeteria because my eye caught movement. A trail of boys filed into the line, and I recognized one of them as our mutual friend. But, it was the guy in the black and yellow App State hoodie with his hat on backward that caught my heart. He was cute.

"Who is that walking with TK?" I asked Lindsay quickly.

"Oh, that's Mark. We met him in TK's room when our internet was down, remember?" I, in fact, did not remember. I was too busy checking my emails and AIM messages to compute his existence back in August.

As soon as I got back to our room, I had Lindsay find him on Facebook through TK's friend list. "This is him...Mark Outten," she sat back to reveal her screen. I scrolled through his page, noticing his dark brown hair, captivating blue eyes, and his interests.

"Oh! He's Christian!" He had my heart at cute *and* Christian.

I added him to my Facebook friends and waited. He added me back, and we began talking through Messenger at first. He was clueless that I liked him at all, seeing that he had never had a girlfriend before. One time I hinted that I wanted to watch the Left Behind movies, and he replied simply, "You should watch it sometime." He clearly missed the opportunity to ask me out to see the movies with him and the DVDs he already owned. Clueless, I tell you!

Yet, somehow, I guess I made my hints even more obvious, or he decided to take a risk, and we decided to meet up in person. Our first meeting was a lunch together where I brought Lindsay and another friend to help be my support system. Thank God they came, because I apparently didn't speak hardly a word. I was terribly shy. They asked him questions, and I just ate my pot roast spud with blushing cheeks.

We both were shy people, and it's truly a miracle that we ended up married one day. I guess on Messenger we could more easily speak beyond our in-person awkwardness, so that may have laid a foundation for us. The written word has always come more naturally for me when it comes to expressing myself. Later that week, we decided to try a real date, with us both probably petrified about how to talk to one another. He picked me up wearing a baby blue plaid button down short sleeve shirt and his signature cargo jeans, and I wore a sweater. The gorgeous, colorful, and cool-aired fall of the mountains was beginning to arrive around us.

We settled into a hard wooden booth for dinner at Macado's in downtown Boone. Sitting across from each other, we both ordered chicken tenders like the new adults we were and slowly warmed up to conversation. We talked about our families, what it was like growing up, where we were from, and all kinds of things. I remember feeling connected that though we grew up differently, there still were similarities. His dad was in the Air Force, so he moved around every three years or so, just like me. While I wasn't in a military family, he understood what it was like to start over and over making new friends while being shy and the insecurities that follow.

I didn't tell him about Kaylee though just yet. I didn't want to scare him away with a quick judgment of my character and actions before the Lord changed my life. I wanted him to know who I was *now* first. Still, it was scary to know I was holding this secret (from everyone at college, actually, for the same reason) and that I would reveal it soon. *Would it change things?* Dating after placement was new for me, and I had waited to take it seriously. Though I had a few interests from time to time since I was sixteen, they never became boyfriends. For two years, I had kept my heart guarded and waiting. Something within me told me Mark was different, and his character over time would continue to reveal that. He didn't try to kiss me. He didn't make a move. He was perfectly chivalrous, with a calm and patient presence about him that felt steady.

On our second date, we decided to attend CRU together, Campus Crusade For Christ, which led worship and shared a message every Thursday. After that, we stopped by his dorm for a blanket to sit on and walked to the football field nearby to stargaze. He stretched out his plush buttercream blanket for us, and we took our seats beside one another. We didn't cozy up or even hold hands. We just talked.

Eventually, Mark looked at me with a sheepish grin, "You know, this might be kind of obvious, but I like you."

"I like you, too."

My heart was full of hope, and since I wanted to move forward with our relationship, I knew he needed to know something important first. It was here under the twinkling stars in the dips of the surrounding mountains that I told him about Kaylee.

Once I was finished explaining, his response was, "Well, God forgives you, and I do, too."

Maybe that seems to be an odd statement to others, but to me, it was a relief. Since I could already picture a future with Mark, having his forgiveness for giving my heart and body away to others meant a lot. He wasn't judging me or scared away. I was accepted, baggage and all.

For the next several weeks, we still took our time to get to know each other. We didn't call ourselves boyfriend and girlfriend just yet, even though we liked each other. We didn't kiss. I was trying so hard to do things differently this time. For a while, that worked, but once we did officially decide to date, compromises slowly began to happen. Living at college with no accountability or supervision made that too easy. We both were caught in the familiar tension between being drawn to one another and shame that I knew too well.

Over Christmas break, Mark told his parents, "This is the girl I want to marry. I can feel it." His parents knew about Kaylee and were equally accepting of her and my past. They extended grace and understanding, which was also relieving. Of course, they told him to slow down and enjoy college.

My soul knew, too: *This is him!* We dreamed of what our future would look like, with two kids (ha!) and wanting to raise our family in one place—something neither of us had growing up. We couldn't wait to begin forever together.

We often visited our different families on some weekends to have more time together and get to know our future in-laws. One weekend when Mark was visiting for dinner, my mom whispered to me out of earshot, "You think maybe he's the one?"

I nodded in agreement with a knowing smile. She could see the difference and the love we shared as well, even with it being a new relationship and still being only eighteen.

I told Christine and Phil as well that I had met an amazing guy, and they welcomed him into their home for a visit when Kaylee was eighteen months old. Seeing him play with her, accept her, and getting their stamp of approval on him made me fall in love with Mark even more.

As the semester passed, we shared our first Valentines Day, spring break, and many other relationship firsts. We rarely fought, but when we did, we quickly worked it out. He was patient with me through my anxious attachment that constantly needed approval and attention to make sure we were good. He taught me a lot about myself, and God used him in a lot of ways to mature me. Our personalities balance each other well.

In June, Kaylee celebrated her second birthday, and Mark's parents even sent gifts for her. Shortly after though, I knew something was up. I had a babysitting job for the summer, and I kept dozing off when we would watch TV in the early hours before playing. I also suddenly craved pizza and ranch, which is and has always been repulsive to me. Once my period was two days late, I took a pregnancy test.

Positive. Again. Two years after Kaylee. *Here we go again.*

I felt the familiar shock of seeing two pink lines staring back at me, along with the excitement of having a baby. While I was only eighteen, I still knew I was more ready this time around. Having Mark by my side was a huge emotional stabilizer, and being legally an adult made me feel more equipped.

Still, I knew this would shatter our worlds again at first and that we would need support. I felt deeply the assurance that the Lord would work all the details out of how we would provide for this child, and that He would bring excitement for this baby within our family over time. While Mark and I made a mistake and would face the natural consequences of that, this baby was already so loved and desired.

Yet, I braced myself for the impact of the disappointment to come. The first person I told aside from Mark was my mom.

"Well, I think you are just meant to be a mom." And that was that with her; she became my most supportive person to lean on when another storm was brewing.

When we told each of our families, it truthfully was one of the worst moments of my life, right up there with signing Kaylee's relinquishment papers. This time there wasn't the same grace extended. Shame filled me. I apologized profusely. There were "How could you let this happen again?" and "Don't you see that you are still in the same place you were two years ago?" comments from many family members. I felt like I had ruined Mark and his seemingly perfect bubble of a life. I accepted my part in my mistake and was sorry, but I also had my stubborn faith that God blessed us with this child and it would all work out.

Of course, another hard conversation was telling Kaylee's parents. I was terrified that this would ruin the relationship we had built. Would this be a changing factor so that they couldn't trust my character any longer? Would it shut down our open adoption? Would they see me as a bad influence? I don't remember exactly how it went or what I said, but I do remember being met with grace. Phil sat across the long dining room table where we often had our heartfelt chats.

With his caring eyes and fatherly voice, he offered, "You and Mark have our full support, but if you decide to choose adoption again, we would love to keep both kids together and adopt this baby."

While adoption wasn't what we felt was best for this baby— a deep knowing just as I had known adoption was best for Kaylee— I appreciated that they would have been willing. They assured me that our relationship wasn't in jeopardy but that they wanted to make sure that we create a steady life because Kaylee would be watching and looking up to me. I agreed and told them I would. I still wanted to make her proud. I wanted her to see that even though we make mistakes, we can get back up, and the Lord can bring beauty from it.

FALLING INTO PLACE

One natural consequence was having to leave the college we loved, Appalachian State. I had been all set to move in with Jessica into an apartment and had to break our lease. It broke Mark's and my hearts to give up the mountains. He enrolled at UNC Charlotte near his parents and began working a part-time job to save up for our new little family.

As for me, I was no longer welcome to live at my dad's house. And, I didn't want to move back in with my mom because I wanted to preserve the good relationship we had developed, plus it was hours away from Mark. Because we wanted to get married, we didn't want a long distance relationship. So, I decided to move into a maternity home called Lois' Lodge 30 minutes away from Mark. Gray was still in my life, helping me through this new situation. She helped me apply and get set up.

Lois' Lodge was a Christian home, and I genuinely was excited to move in and get back on track. At our interview, I told them how desperately I wanted to be a good mother and wife. I wanted to learn how to cook, clean, do finances, and grow my relationship in the Lord. It was a fresh start, again, and a step into independence as I prepared for motherhood and marriage.

There were many wonderful things about being there, from the deep friendships made with the other girls in similar situations to the care from the community that lavished us with food, pampering days, and gifts. We went to church together and had a weekly Bible Study that really deepened my understanding of God's characteristics. While I still had a lot of family tensions to work through, it felt good to redirect my life toward changing and growing yet again.

It was a rule that you had to either be in school or working, so I decided to pursue a job. What started out as a temporary job in August 2006 at an event planning organization for Bank of America turned into a job lasting my entire pregnancy. They kept extending my job because of my doing well and my work ethic. That felt good. I felt like an adult with my business professional attire over my growing belly and with making good money. I saved as much as I could, which helped pay for our wedding and set us up as a new family. That job was such a blessing from the Lord and the best thing that came from Lois' Lodge.

Still, it wasn't always easy living there. There were rules that seemed absurd, one being that Mark and I couldn't see each other often simply because it wasn't fair to the other girls living there who didn't have their baby's fathers in their lives. How were we supposed to build a strong relational foundation for marriage?

Mark would often come to appointments with me when his schedule allowed, or we would have lunch together. My job was one way that we skirted around the home's rules. Together, we learned that this child was a girl and named her Savannah Leigh.

In October, we took a trip together, again, skirting around the home's rules. We did go see my mom as I said I was, but we made a stop in Boone first. I stayed with Jessica, and he stayed with his buddy, Josh. That Saturday morning we took a drive with Josh to Beacon Heights, a short hike with a beautiful view off the parkway. I was hangry that morning and needed food desperately, so much so that Josh likely questioned what Mark was about to do. After getting breakfast, we made our way to the top, and Mark proposed, Josh watching behind a bush nearby. It was surreal that it was finally happening! Our little family was coming together, and our future was beginning. I couldn't wait to marry him, yet we agreed on a wedding date in May because I didn't want to be pregnant at our wedding.

In December, my parents and online friends threw me a surprise baby shower. I was right that as time moved forward, their hearts would become accepting and joyful about this arrival. My Adoptions of Love crew even made the trip from states away and literally provided every need for Savannah. I was floored at all the love and support and grateful that time was turning this situation around to be a celebration and not a disappointment.

As my pregnancy was nearing its end in January— I was due in February— I began to worry about where I would go once Savannah was born. Lois' Lodge had a separate house for moms and kids, but only for a limited time, and it still was thirty minutes away from Mark. My mom's house was an option, but she was hours away, and again it would separate Mark and me even more when we needed to be together as parents.

As I stressed and worried, I felt the Lord assure my heart. *Trust me, Mark's parents will change their minds. You'll have a home with them.* Peace washed over me, and I just waited for God's timing. Sure enough, two weeks later they invited me into their home to live.

"The more we thought about it, the more we felt like you needed to be here. Mark is this baby's father, and he needs to be around for her and for you."

Relief and joy flooded my heart. We would finally be together as a family! I praised the Lord for fulfilling His promise and making a way.

I moved in just before Super Bowl Sunday, with the rule that Mark and I would have separate bedrooms until marriage. Time quickly passed, and my induction was set for February 22, 2007. Her birth story was very similar to Kaylee's, and at 9:22 pm, Savannah was born. Weeping as I held her for the first time, Mark by my side, I couldn't believe she was all mine. I was a mother. Though Savannah will never replace the spot in my heart reserved for Kaylee, it was a layer of healing to know that I could still experience the moments of motherhood that I worried I would never have. I felt blessed. Even if things were out of the traditional order, we were blessed.

My family and Mark's family were there for support and to get us set up as new parents. I learned to nurse her through tears and pain but clinging to the desire to want to breastfeed no matter what. Mark and I would share nighttime duty those early days, with me sleeping a stretch while he kept her entertained while playing Xbox, and then switching when she wanted to nurse again. We were learning to become a team, and it was beautiful. Mark's parents were also a help since they were home and retired. When I desperately needed a nap, they would offer to hold her. Yet, I often would try not to ask for help. I wanted to prove to others that I could be a good mom and do things myself.

Another beautiful thing during this time was that since I had moved into Mark's house, I was only minutes away from Kaylee and her family. They were preparing to move two hours away, but for a short time, we were close. Surprisingly, we didn't see each other as much as you would think, largely due to my figuring out how to be a mom and planning a wedding, plus their own busy lives. But when we did, I loved seeing my two girls together. Kaylee was enthralled with Savannah, yet in a typical sibling way also became frustrated when Savannah would do things like chew on Kaylee's fancy dress up! They met on the day Savannah came home from the hospital and have been best friends since.

Slowly, the Lord worked out every detail to provide for our family and heal heart wounds. We married on a chilly spring day, May 19th, 2007, surrounded by the Boone mountains we loved, family and friends. It was small and low budget, but

I was proud of what we had pulled together debt-free and with the help of my Nanny. Kaylee was there with her family, and Savannah was three months old being passed around to adoring people. It was perfect for us. After our honeymoon in Wilmington, NC, we made our room together in a large bonus room above his parents' garage.

Mark continued with his classes, and the Lord soon provided a well-paying internship at a large energy company. Graduation led to a full time job which still provides well for us as a family sixteen years later, enough so that I can be home with our kids!

I went back to work part-time during the summer when Savannah was a few months old with Mark's parents watching her during those hours, but by the end of summer, his dad encouraged me to think about going back to school.

"If you wait too long, you might not ever go back. We would like to watch Savannah so that you can finish your degree, too."

With that encouragement, I quit my job and applied to UNC Charlotte. This time, I pursued an English degree, as I had discovered social work classes were not my expertise, but writing was. My dad even said to me during freshman year at App Sate, "Leah, I think you should switch to English; you're a great writer and getting good grades in those classes." I distinctly remember being in our kitchen and how touched I was that he noticed and was encouraging me. When my quiet dad talks, you know to listen! My college professor at App made the same remarks when I turned in my essays, "You are a writer, Leah." So with this new chapter of college, I sought out a path that would enhance and grow the natural talent I was told I had.

I applied for FAFSA grants, and the Lord blew us away again. Since Mark and I were married and had a dependent, we qualified for several grants and scholarships, which made attending college absolutely free for both of us for the rest of our college careers. It even provided book money and extra to live off of. Wow! While Savannah came at a different time than we envisioned, the Lord was blessing our obedience in giving her life and walking His path as a family together.

Having Savannah actually improved my grades since I was forced to study and work hard during her naptime, at night, or in the computer lab during school days between classes. Each semester, I arranged my classes so that I only went into school two full days a week and had five days home with her. This worked well to balance both needing a break as a mom and being with Savannah as much as possible. Many days, Mark and I shared those days on campus together, which gave us time during our commute and lunch breaks to spend together. It was a cherished time, though busy and difficult, too. I couldn't wait to be done with school and be a stay-at-home mom!

For three years, we lived with Mark's parents as we finished our degrees, and Mark began his full time job. While it wasn't always easy, it was a gift of time and their support to build our own solid foundation as a family and financially. In the spring of 2010 at the age of 22, we bought our first little house thirty minutes from Mark's parents, and I graduated with honors.

My blog had grown and I had begun to get paid advertisements and products to review as a little extra on the side, which eventually turned into freelance writing. Writing was still a personal way to navigate my feelings, but as a young mom, it also became an outlet to do something just for me. The Lord used this gift He bestowed in multiple ways over the years.

We settled into our townhome and I began my stay-at-home life, making playdates and friends in our community. We found a church and loved where we lived. It wasn't long after moving in that I saw another stick with two pink lines, and Jaxson joined our family in my first natural birth with a midwife. Two years later Ashlyn came into the world in our bedroom, followed by Sadie, and eventually Lylah.

We had only planned two kids, but each time I felt a nudge from the Lord. *Do you really trust me? There's another one for your family.*

We had to move into a larger house to fit us all, but with each step, the Lord paved the way. We weren't perfect, of course. We were still figuring out how to be adults, how to be married, how to communicate better, and how to love one another in our unique ways, but we kept fighting for us. Mark and I have been determined to be the stable family that I always wanted growing up. Now he jokes as our kids fight over who gets to sit by me that they make up for all the love I didn't feel as a child at times.

While I've had seasons of postpartum depression and working through my own childhood traumas to be a better mom for my children, each child has helped me to press into the Lord to meet their needs. We aim to be a home that is filled with never-ending love, a safe place for emotions, and a presence of peace. He's brought the promise of a family into life far beyond what I could dream it could be.

CHAPTER 9

Sweeter (and More Complex) With Time

During the first three years, Kaylee's family and I continued to intensively build our relationship and maintained visits, often once a month, right up until they moved a few hours away when Savannah was six months old.

Those first three years laid the foundation for the trust, respect, and honor that we felt for one another. It helped establish good communication and friendship between us so that as things shifted in our lives, we still had a solid foundation to stand on. We established fun traditions that carried on throughout her childhood and into her teen years.

Most importantly, as Kaylee grew to understand and feel more about her adoption or question her identity, that foundation we built became a strong place for her to land. That, to me, is the goal of open adoption. She has both families as a support, which creates a steady footing to launch into adulthood.

As I walked this new path as both a birth mom and a new young mom, naturally, I wrestled with many emotions. On one hand, I felt still felt peace and joy in my relationship with Kaylee and being a part of each other's lives. I was able to experience so many memories with her, far more than I imagined would be possible. On the other hand was grief.

Experiencing motherhood with Savannah was a reminder of the little things I had missed with Kaylee. For me, my role as birth mother has and will always be a balance of gratefulness and grief.

As the years went by, our adoption relationship had many ebbs and flows based on the season we were in. Yet, our promises remained to one another to keep Kaylee's best interest and Jesus at the center of our relationship.

THE ELEMENTARY YEARS

As Kaylee began elementary school and I was immersed in my growing family, our visits spread out to two times a year. It happened naturally, simply a result of busy seasons for all of us. We had built a strong foundation the first three years and now we're building our lives more separately. As Kaylee grew and I healed, I didn't need as much connection and communication as the previous years. I loved that her dad would call me with a funny story, or her mom would tell me how much her eyes looked like mine. Yet, our basic agreement was always honored and upheld. There still were emails and calls with updates and our two traditional visits.

Every birthday we were invited, and every Christmas we had our special party. It usually fell the same weekend every December, and I felt grateful that each year her parents would set that day apart for us. It was one small way that affirmed our importance as Kaylee's birth family. If we needed to adjust the date or location due to an issue like when we needed to move into a new house on that weekend, or a global pandemic we would, but usually it was the same. All of my parents and siblings would come, along with grandparents, aunts, and cousins from her adoptive family side. It felt like a wonderful reunion of a uniquely blended family every year. We always felt accepted into their family.

Our very first Christmas, we met halfway at a Japanese restaurant, and that remained the meeting place for lunch nearly every year. Eventually, they moved a few minutes away from the restaurant, so we were able to extend our party after lunch to their house and added a Dirty Santa game for the adults to exchange gifts. Back then, there were a huge amount of adults and children, so it made giving gifts easier! Kaylee's family always gave me a gift though, and items with Kaylee's photo on them were always a favorite.

Most of our visits consisted of the kids running off to play while I sat with her parents to hear updates and the newest funny Kaylee story. My love for her was deep, but my closeness was still with her parents. It was easier to know her through them than to know her directly at this age full of energy. Occasionally I would get a chance to sneak a one-on-one moment with her while we played. I remember when she was around five, I believe I had just attended her Kindergarten graduation, and I went upstairs to tell her goodbye. As she sat on the carpet with her Barbie dolls, she casually began to tell *me* why I chose adoption for *her*. Her parents have always done a great job of talking positively about adoption and birth family in their home, just as they had promised. Kaylee matter-a-factually proclaimed while smoothing her Barbie's blonde hair, "You were young when you had me and couldn't take care of me, so you chose my mommy and daddy." It was simple and perfect for a five-year-old. Over the years, those conversations would grow. But, both Kaylee and I have been grateful for how adoption and me being her birth mom was always part of her normal. I will never forget the time I walked through the restaurant door for a Christmas visit, and she yelled, "MY BIRTH MOM!" It was evidence that they talked about me, and it meant the world that she knew my role in her life and wanted to see me.

It was during the elementary years that I felt more distant from Kaylee, with less visits and more awkward interactions in which I didn't always know what to do or say to connect with her. I realized I didn't know her favorite foods, her best friend, what she loved to watch, or really, her favorite of anything. As a mom of several kids at this point, that hurt because I knew my parented kids well. Kaylee's parents knew her in this way, but I didn't know Kaylee well. Eventually, when Kaylee was around age nine, that changed when she started to process adoption more. For the first time, she asked to stay at our house for the night. Since we had years of building a relationship and her parents knew my home and my family well, it was a natural next step for us. They knew we were safe and that she would be cared for well.

I planned this time to intentionally get to know Kaylee and lean into what I did know already. We did crafts and watched a movie. She snuggled with her tiny siblings. We made sheet forts, and I discovered she *loves* my tacos. Those sleepovers at our house became our new summer tradition, starting with one night and extending longer each year.

THE TEEN YEARS

Christine and I stood between our cars after loading in Kaylee's purple polka dot suitcase. As the summer breeze flipped around our hair she relayed instructions, "She got a phone for her thirteenth birthday; we will see how it goes. But, she has it in case she needs us for anything. Please make sure she doesn't lose it and that she brushes her teeth."

Kaylee was coming to stay a whole week this time with us, per her request, as this new birthday visit tradition kept expanding each year to try longer periods of time together. This gift of a longer time together was a new favorite of all of ours— including my parented children. All five adore their biggest sister and look forward to her visits. So much so that we've had to schedule one-on-one time with each sibling some years so that she's not fought over! A whole week meant more time to pack in fun, like board games, snow cones, shopping, and the pool.

Mark has always supported my relationship with Kaylee, and as he joined in on many of our visits starting when she was eighteen months old, he became a "fun uncle" type of person in her life. He's always goofed around with her and initiated family activities. They lovingly pick on each other and both have a love for board games. My role has always felt more like an Aunt role as well but with a maternal instinct. We genetically look alike and have personality similarities, and we look forward to our time together. Yet, I'm not her mom. I'm a support person in her life. I love her fiercely like a mother, just as with all my children. Because of open adoption, I can mother her in my own way, while fully respecting and honoring her mom's important role.

Kaylee getting a phone also marked the beginning of us developing our own relationship deeper. For the first time, I had direct contact with her to ask her questions or to answer hers or just to say, "Hey, I'm thinking of you, and I love you!" For the first thirteen years, her parents were the gatekeepers, and through our friendship, I found out most of my information about Kaylee with new updates, fun stories, and arranging visits. Turning thirteen marked Kaylee having more say in our relationship. The fact that Kaylee chooses me back, that she wants to know me more and wants to spend time with us... I'm grateful. Not every adoptee has this desire or feels safe to express a need for their birth family, but Kaylee has been given a safe place to share her feelings and desires. That's a testament to her parents' way of open-hearted parenting.

Each year from there, we continued to treasure these summer visits, exploring different lengths of time and adding new adventures together. She wanted more time— a week wasn't enough to fully settle into our world. There was an undeniable awkwardness when we first started our visits for many years, even with all our time together. *Does she want a hug? Does she feel comfortable asking for what she needs? Does she feel like she fits in with us?* Just when she started to feel comfortable and a part of our family, it was time to go back home. So we tried visiting for two weeks per her request. And some years, returning again for a second visit in the summer. We followed her lead, and if we could make a visit work, we would make it happen.

Her parents were always supportive and said, "We much rather her be there and playing than sitting at home in her room while we work." Still, these longer visits came with adjustments when she went back home. Something not talked about much within open adoption is the emotional adjustment it can be for birth families and adoptees when returning back to our lives separately. There are extreme highs and joys as we are so excited to spend this time together, but sometimes when we part ways again, it's difficult. Kaylee has shared that there is a sense of belonging at our house driven by genetics like desiring similar flavors of foods, having similar interests, or how we do things, and it feels different when returning home. It's like that primal wound is ripped open again. When we are together we feel whole, and then when we say "goodbye for now," we feel it at our core. Kaylee has shared with me that it was more difficult when she was younger and our visits were more spread out. She also shared that the longer the visit we had, the longer she needed to decompress. Yet, for us, the joy of knowing each other and the time spent making memories far outweigh the grief it may trigger after.

In her teen years, we all learned to expect this cycle and to allow time and space to process after a visit ended if needed. For me, our visits have always helped to have new memories made to hold onto and to look forward to what's next. It's kept me moving forward in healing. But, of course, at times I feel sad when it's time to go home because I miss her for the person she is, just like I miss my children's presence when they go to a grandparents' house to stay— only our separation is much longer. It's always been worth it, though, to maintain our visits, and neither of us would change how we have approached our time together. The joy outweighs the grief. And, having technology like texting and video calling helps in between.

For most of Kaylee's teenage years, we maintained our two traditional visits each year with lots of family involved, along with our new summer visit tradition. But, we also added new ways of visiting now that she was older. We began a bucket list of firsts that we wanted to experience together. We took our first trips together like to the beach, to visit Asheville and the Biltmore House, snow tubing, and leaf gazing in the mountains.

One of our favorite memories together was going to see We The Kingdom in concert, a Christian band we both love. Instead of a physical gift for Christmas when she was seventeen, I wanted to gift us an experience to do together. I checked the dates with her parents and booked VIP tickets where we got to meet the band, attend a Q&A, and have front row seats. Her excitement was worth every penny that I splurged on this experience! We enjoyed screaming songs together and cried at the songs that touched our hearts. But, by far the best part about it was the surreal honor of worshiping wholeheartedly next to the daughter who was growing in my tummy when Jesus came knocking at my heart's door.

Over the years we kept adding to our "firsts" together. I watched my kids have their first snowball fight, their first real sibling argument, our first official family photo with her included, and the first time I got to care for her when she was sick during a visit. There even was a time that I was able to pick her up from school her senior year— a first and a last— but I'm so glad I could have that experience. Normal, everyday firsts have often been on our bucket list, even more than the grander things like trips. Everyday moments are what I grieve and miss the most— but with open adoption, we get to experience some of them in our own way.

In the early teen years, it was a lot of family time with her immersed in our busy home full of young children. That was beneficial for all of us, especially all my children in building their bond together. We all enjoyed this time together, but it typically meant that Kaylee and I got barely any good quality time together. She desired more time, as did I. As she grew into an older teen, she used her voice and said, "Six months between visits is too long. I think it would help me to see you once each season." So we made an adjustment again to fit her needs and for what worked for all of us. We decided to aim for quarterly visits with a mix of family time and one-on-one time. Summer and winter were with family, and it often ended up that in spring and fall, I was able to come to visit her at her house for a weekend together.

Sometimes her parents were home during those short weekend visits, and it reminded me of the days when she was a baby and we sat around their kitchen table talking for hours, except this time she sat with us and talked, too. Other times, her parents went away on a trip for a weekend and asked if I would stay with her and help care for their dogs. Those weekends were equally as amazing as the longer visits, they just looked different. We were able to talk more openly about our feelings and we could plan intentional time together doing what we wanted.

One weekend, I went to visit her when she was sixteen, and I planned a day for us to show her places of my past— where her story began. We packed snacks and made our way to the mountain where God opened my eyes. As we hiked the short distance to the outlook, this time with Kaylee beside me rather than within me, it became a full circle moment. At sixteen she was standing in the exact place I stood when I was sixteen. Just as the Lord unveiled my eyes here, He helped her understand through this view of my perspective. She felt how young sixteen still feels, how nervous I had to have been, how unprepared, and how desperately I wanted her life to be different from my own.

On our way home, we drove past the high school I attended with her birth father. We drove by his old townhouse and the places we used to go together. I took her to see my old house, where my stepfather (though now divorced from my mother) still lives. The same peacock green car he drove me to dance classes in still sat in the driveway. The brick ranch with blue shutters, gravel driveway, and overgrown yard looked exactly the same. It felt like going back in time to my own sixteenth year.

My stepfather was always kind and supportive to me when he and my mom were married, even through Kaylee's pregnancy. I thought, *Why not say hi and introduce Kaylee?* So, I rang the doorbell. He was shocked to see us standing there on his tiny brick porch, understandably, but he let us in with a welcome. Everything looked exactly the same aside from more clutter, some new furniture, and new cobwebs dangling from ceiling corners. I was able to show her my old room, which was now his office. Kaylee could see for herself why I didn't want to raise a child here. Back then, it wasn't just the emotional environment of tension between me and my mom; it was the physical environment, too. The house felt old and dirty. I wanted her to have a clean home and so much more. Though she has known her story and "my why" for as long as she could remember, she understood my choice even more deeply. On this day, she saw my perspective with her own eyes. Kaylee shared with me that this day helped her to see how far I've come. Because today, my life looks very different. She sees me thriving. She never would have imagined the life I had lived and who I was before. Adoption truly had been a second chance for both of us to break many cycles.

BEGINNING THE ADULT YEARS

In 2022, Kaylee turned eighteen and graduated high school all in the same weekend. I felt like I did most of my grieving of this huge milestone in the months leading up to it, much like when I was pregnant with her. I felt the weight of all the years, the daily moments missed, the choice I felt I had to make to better our lives— yet also still felt the present peace of the Lord and gratitude for everything we do have together. What a beautiful redemption in all that God has done in my life, her life, and our story. How amazing that we are all still here, surrounding her in love.

I wasn't the one who chose her schools or packed her lunch. I didn't have to struggle to get her there on time or to get homework done. I wasn't the one who took her shopping for the first day of school outfits or backpacks. I only took her to school and picked her up in the carline one time, while her family did every day. I didn't get the car ride conversations daily or take care of her on sick days... but I chose the parents who did. And they did amazingly. Everything I prayed for, both in raising her and for our open adoption, they delivered above and beyond. How like God that she would turn eighteen and graduate on the same weekend. The day she walked across that stage was also the day eighteen years before I had signed relinquishment papers, fully entrusting Kaylee to her family. What a full circle moment. When blessing our food later that day at her celebration, her dad said, "None of this would have been possible without Leah. Thank you." And while this time wasn't really about me, the honor they have always given me continues to help me feel seen, valued, and an important part of their lives simply because I am her birth mother. It helps my aches to know that my loss for their gain isn't invisible.

Turning eighteen is a milestone many adoptees and birth mothers eagerly await, especially if they are hoping for a reunion after a closed adoption, or a new level of contact after only letters for years. For us in a fully open adoption, it added a new sense of freedom for Kaylee to have even more of a voice in what she desired and make more of her own decisions. With high school done and now enrolled in online college classes, Kaylee had the freedom to visit us in new ways. In fact, she asked to live with us for an "extended visit" of a few months. She wanted to immerse herself in our home and our world. She desired to know all of her siblings here deeper, and she hoped for more quiet moments with me while the kids were at school. She wanted to be included as family, even down to the chore chart.

While this was something I could have only dreamed of and hoped for as a birth mom, I was painfully aware of how this had to feel for her adoptive parents. The "giver" was now receiving. In an odd way, we were switching places for a season. They were supportive of the plan, but I can imagine it wasn't always easy for them. They were sharing her back with me in a most unusual way that many adoptive parents would never agree to... yet they did. They agreed it was a good time in life to explore her biological roots more and stretch her wings out to be a tad more independent yet in a safe place. We had expectations set and a plan in place. I couldn't help but think about eighteen years ago when we sat around the dinner table dreaming of what our relationship would look like when she was older, preparing for the days when she wanted to come to me... we were now living it out. I know what it's like to share and give pieces of your heart, wanting to do what's best for your child even if it hurts. I appreciate their prioritization of what Kaylee needs, even now as an adult. I never, ever have wanted to step on their toes as her parents or to take their place. They are just as important in her life as I am, so I have tried hard to maintain that into adulthood, even as she is leaning into me even more.

In October, before she moved in, I prepared the guest room for her as a surprise, taking note of styles she posted on Instagram and knowing her favorite colors. A white net canopy hung over the bed, pink flowers were draped over the headboard, and soft green curtains hung over the windows. There was a desk for her to do art. For the first time, all six of my children had a space of their own and would be under my care for a season. Sixteen-year-old Leah would be absolutely astonished if she peeked into the future.

With eighteen years of visits, you would think we would be totally comfortable with one another, but no. There was still an awkwardness between us—wanting to be close emotionally and physically but not sure how to bridge that gap. Kaylee living with us for months helped build that bridge. It was a natural progression that evolved our relationship to be more authentic.

The first six weeks were incredible and went smoothly with no major issues. We spent many mornings drinking hot chai tea before doing schoolwork. We had more space and time to talk about anything and everything. She was eager to help around the house and enjoyed time with her siblings. Yet, as the darker days of late fall arrived, we felt a shift. We both have a tendency towards seasonal depression, and with the growing stresses of school for her, and for me to make sure I was meeting her parents' expectations, it became more challenging at times. After six weeks, it felt like she truly settled into our home, and I saw more of what her parents described about issues at home. I became more annoyed at little things, just like with any person you live with eventually, and we got on her nerves, too. We had moved beyond polite guests to real life. For the first time ever, we got mad at each other! Our masks we've held onto came down. We stepped off the high pedestal we had placed each other on, a new level of closeness reached.

In allowing her to move in with us, I was fearful of what conflict and "real life" would do to our relationship. Would she begin to hate me and not want to spend time here? Would she regret moving in? Would seeing me at my stressed worst as a mom make her see me differently? The reality is, being mad at each other made us work through, communicate, and grow deeper in the process, just like in any important relationship. Being able to be mad in a safe place is a beautiful thing. It helped our awkwardness, too. We are now able to talk and be human with less of a filter, just like with my other kids.

Kaylee agrees, "The awkwardness between us has changed so much with time. I feel like I can come to you and talk without being nervous. Staying with you helped me get out of my shell and for me be more real."

Two major holidays fell within her extended time in our home and Kaylee was able to decide where she wanted to spend them for the first time ever. She desired to experience a big family Thanksgiving and Christmas, especially with younger siblings that would be excited for Christmas morning. Her parents were understanding of this desire, even if it was hard for them to switch plans for the year. It was purely her decision, though, of course, we hoped to experience our first holiday with her as well. For weeks she went over the pros and cons, sharing how torn she felt having to decide. She felt guilty for wanting to be with us and didn't want to hurt anyone's feelings. I understood that myself, as a child who felt torn between my dad's side and my mom's growing up, and even now sometimes I feel this way as an adult. Ultimately, she decided this was the ideal time to celebrate with us since she was already here, and it truly seemed like the Lord paved the way with surrounding circumstances.

Our first Thanksgiving was spent at my dad's and Cyndi's house, and it was everything I ever hoped for, and she agrees. We spent the day prior to Thanksgiving preparing the food with my stepmom with aprons on and music playing in the kitchen. The next day, she had a Thanksgiving meal sitting at our table with our traditional foods, foods she would have grown up eating had she lived with us. We watched our traditional Thanksgiving movies, the parade, and ate lots of treats, including the Strawberry Pretzel Salad I had craved when she was still in my belly. It's hard to put into words how thankful we were to have her presence with us, even if it is for only one year. It was the best Thanksgiving ever.

She decided to stay for Christmas as well, and we were thrilled to experience more firsts together. I bought our family all matching Christmas PJ's, and for the first time, she was able to be included. We decorated the house together with Christmas music softly playing. We went Christmas shopping together to find gifts for her siblings and parents. We wrapped gifts together. Unfortunately, after that, nothing went how it typically does for Christmas since most of our family got sick, including Kaylee. Being sick thwarted our plans and shifted things. Our annual tour-de-lights was moved, and our usual Christmas morning was a little less energetic and with less extended family around to join us. We didn't get to experience a normal Christmas as we hoped to show Kaylee, but she was here, and that was enough.

Being sick around the holidays, and now being months away from home, was the signal she needed to end her extended visit. She wasn't just sick, she was homesick. She missed her parents, her dogs, and her friends. I made her mom's southern chicken stew to help her feel better and bring some of her mom's comfort here one day. But, after the holiday chaos and being exhausted from sickness, we knew it was time to say goodbye-for-now once more. Of course, there was an adjustment for all of us, especially for my children at home, but our hearts were also overflowing with the joy of all that we were blessed to experience together.

After Kaylee returned home, our closeness has remained. While our season together wasn't always easy, we are both grateful that it led to many firsts and a deeper connection. I was scared that any conflict would put a wedge between us, yet we have only grown closer. Our relationship has only become even more of a safe place for one another.

CHAPTER 10

The Best is Yet to Come

Years ago, when Kaylee was still in elementary school and I knew her less personally, and when my soul ached a bit more, I kept feeling the Lord whisper hope to me: "The best is yet to come." I had hope that everything we have today would be our story, but I balanced this hope delicately with the reality that it might not be so. Still, I felt the Lord give me glimpses to cling to, and now we are living this hope beyond what I could have dreamed.

I have always felt immensely blessed by our adoption relationship, and each year I am left in awe that it keeps getting better. Do we navigate hard moments and emotions? Does it have layers of complexity? Absolutely, but overall, we have a deep love for each other and a desire to keep going and make it work for Kaylee's good.

So what's next? This. More of this life together! More of Kaylee and I growing and discovering who we are as people. More deep conversations, nose crinkles when we smile, and lighthearted laughter that sounds oddly the same at times. More watching movies and doing crafts together. More trips. More bucket list items being checked off. More processing our emotions and feelings together. More get-togethers with her entire family, birth and adopted.

More birthdays together. Being at her wedding and witnessing the start of new chapters in her life. Maybe being called Nanny Goose (since she calls me Mother Goose, as all my kids have nicknamed me) when she makes us grandparents. More traditions made and kept.

When I asked Kaylee what she hoped for the future in regards to us, she replied, "My hopes have already been met— I always wanted to feel like a part of your family and to be a sibling among your children, and I do!" I feel the same. I can't wait to see what our future holds as the best may be yet to come, but it's also here right now. We are living it.

As for Samuel and Kaylee's relationship, I'm still praying for there to be growth and connection for them, and I always will. While he has missed many years of her life, his mom has remained as a connection to her biological father's side. For that, I am grateful she has connection to those identity roots as well. When Kaylee was around sixteen, she and Samuel started talking online and have taken baby steps to build a relationship. I hope and pray that the best is yet to come for them, too!

I've felt led to share our open adoption story on multiple platforms over the last years for a few reasons. One, it gives the Lord glory. How our relationship has played out, down to the tiny details of naming her nearly identical names, can only be written by a God who can see the whole picture. A sovereign God. A God who cares. A God who sees. A God who brings peace through the process and healing to pain. I have always prayed that our story would bring hope to those who are hurting. I have prayed that it would bring healing to brokenness. Turn to Him. He can move, heal, and create miracles in your life, too.

Secondly, I have seen the difference stories make in undoing stigmas and changing lives. I pray our story shows what is possible when adoption is done well. When support for birth moms is done well. When open adoption is a new version of a blended family and is embraced as a new normal in our society. I have seen personally how sharing my experiences as a birth mom has helped open adoptive family's hearts to include their child's birth family in the most beautiful ways.

I will keep sharing as the Lord provides me with opportunities. I will keep sharing as the Lord is still writing our adoption story. After all, we are still figuring all of this out as we go, and now open adoption into adulthood is something entirely new! I will keep sharing as the Lord continues to guide us.

The best is yet to come with Kaylee and with how the Lord will use our story. Kaylee and I are dreaming together, not just for our personal lives, but for how the Lord may use us to help the adoption community.

Project Backers

To my Kickstarter backers, this is for you! Without you, this project would not have happened. I thank each and every one of you for believing in this book and supporting me. Every share. Every dollar. Every prayer. Every message of encouragement you sent me. *It mattered.* If I could personally hug each of you, I would. May this book be a message that will add light to this world.

THANK YOU. . .

Absolute Love Adoptions

Adopt Match

Alexia Boone

Alicia Nichols

Amanda Auler

Amy Hutton

Amy Stephens

Ann House

April Greenwood

Ashlyn Aburto

Barbie Garcia

Berkley Pope

Beth Foster

Bethanie Carlson Drew

Braedi

Breanna Black

Brett and Morgan Goins

Brianna Hubbard

Britney Grissom

Carla Lewis

Carla Williams

Charity Carstensen

Chelsea Oheim

Cheryl Harvey

Christen S.

Christian Adoption Consultants

Christina Henry

Christine and Phil

Cindy A.

Claire Culwell

Clare Elizabeth

Claudia C. Wolff

Claudia K.

Cyndi and Vic

Danielle, Laura, Jacob

Debra Mack

Dee

Dr. George Fuller Jr.

Emily Miller

Emily Wright

Evelyn

Faith Choate

Family Life Services
Adoption Agency

Gina R. Briggs ♡

Grace Elliott

Gray Moulton

Hands of Hope PRC

Haven Fogarty

Heidi Glick

Jackie Streeter

Jamie

Janie Hynson

Jay Ishino

Jeanna Aston

Jenna

Jennifer Kachler

Jerusha Kingery

Jessica Cheshier

Jill Thomley

Karen Bland

Kasey

Katherine Gentile

Katy Young

Kelli Mayhorn

Kelly Lessard

Kelly Parker

Kirsten Barber

Kristen Henry

Kristen Sheppard

Kristen Yates

Kristin Putnam

Kristina Miller

Krystal Sieben

Lara Kay

Lindsay Bujorian

Laurie Christine

Lenette Serlo

Lindsay Smith

Lydia Morris

Malorie Elrod

Marta Almansa Esteva

Marybeth Robinson

Megan and Nathan Wood

Megan Tucker

Melanie and
Dwight Stone

Melissa Ohden

Mellisa Lathion

Melody Stoltzfus

Mike Gannon

Mischa

Misty Lynn

Morgan Zichettella
Natalie
Nicole "Coley" Strickland
Niemah
Paula K Weeks
Quiver Full
Adoptions, INC.
Rachel & Aaron Bennett
Raquel McCloud
Rebekah McGee
Rhiannon Gancheff
Sarah Morfeld
Sergey Kochergan
Shannan
Sherri Hall
Shonda Larson

Sonja Franck
Susan Wilson
Terri Palamaras
Tessa Byer
The Privette Family
Thea Barry, in honor
of Mama S
Tiana Phillips
Tiny Hearts Collective
Toni Mcintyre
Tori Shaw
Vicki Colls
Victoria Carberry
Grandpa Lynn
Vivienne Smith

Acknowledgments

My husband, Mark. I would not be who I am today without you, nor would I be where I am in my career. Meeting you at 18 years old was a gift from the Lord, and He has used you in mighty ways to grow and support me. Thanks for being my earthly rock and believing in the ministry God has placed on my heart.

My mom, Evelyn. Thanks for always being my absolute biggest fan and encouraging me to try anything that I wanted to set my mind to. Whether that was art, dance, or writing this book, you've always cheered me on.

My dad and stepmom, Vic and Cyndi. Thank you for being a strong support system throughout my life, no matter what! I wouldn't be who I am today without the unconditional love, family fun, and solid example you've been for me.

All of my children— Kaylee, Savannah, Jaxson, Ashlyn, Sadie, Lylah, and two babies in heaven. Each of you has brought me closer to the Lord in your own unique way. Each of you is a gift and a blessing in my life. I'm proud of all of you! Thank you for the sacrifice of time that you've made space for as I completed this project.

My Grandpa Lynn. The grace felt in your hugs will forever be part of what I remember about you. Thanks for loving me even when I felt most undeserving and always supporting me.

Ms. Dunn. Thank you for encouraging me all those years ago. Your kindness stuck with me and always will. I will always bloom where I am planted thanks to your help!

Kaylee's parents, Christine and Phil. I would not have this story without your open hearts that include me. Thanks for loving me well. As an adoptee told me, our girl is in a web of love, and that's all I ever wanted for her! Thanks for everything you do for her.

My community at school, church, friends, and other extended family. I never once felt the judgment I thought I would receive. Thank you for supporting me, even all these years later.

My Adoptions of Love and Birth Mom Buds ladies. You helped me heal. You gave me a space to share, cry, rejoice, learn, and feel seen. I love and miss all of you!

Thank you to my team at Kingdom Winds Publishing. You've helped make another dream come to reality, and I can't thank you enough!

About the Author

Leah is a birth mother in a fully open adoption and a mother of five that she parents with her husband. She has been writing, speaking, and serving the adoption community since 2004. Her passion for helping others blossoms from the light found within the dark trenches of her life and the support surrounding her. Sharing vulnerably about the beauty and aches as a birth mother, she aims to inspire hope and show how open adoption can be done well. Leah's writing and story have been featured on national platforms including *Focus On The Family*, *Epoch Times*, *LiveAction*, and *HuffPost*.

Leah would love to connect with you! Find her on social media for updates on her story, services she provides, adoption relationship tools, and speaking opportunities.

leahoutten.com
facebook.com/thegracebond
instagram.com/leahoutten

About the Cover Designer

Kaylee is Leah's birth daughter whom she placed when she was sixteen years old. Now a young adult, Kaylee has grown into a talented artist in many types of mediums. With a specialty in digital art, she designed the cover (and named the book!). It was only fitting to ask Kaylee to help with this special project, which isn't just Leah's story, but a part of Kaylee's story as well. Kaylee is currently an art student and commissions artist.

instagram.com/keirichu
illustrationsbykay.my.canva.site
ko-fi.com/keirichu

Bonus Material

PHOTOS

Teen Leah — 16 years old, before I knew I was pregnant

With my new puppy, Chloe, at 9 months pregnant

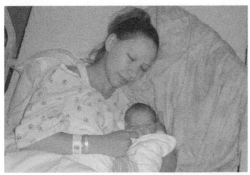

Kaylee and I napping together

Breanna drove 13 hours to be by my side

My parents and I with Phil, Christine, and Kaylee on the day we left the hospital

Kaylee with me and Christine

Celebrating Kaylee's first birthday

Mark meeting Kaylee, then 18 months old, while we were dating

Savannah is born, 2007

Mark and I marry in May 2007. Kaylee & her family attend, age 3

Our Christmas visit 2016

All of my children together, family photos 2020

Kaylee viewing Pilot Mountain; our full circle moment

Kaylee turns 18, 2022

Kaylee graduates, 2022

Kaylee and Savannah on our first Thanksgiving together, 2022